FAITH IN

GOVERNANCE

RENEWING THE ROLE OF THE DIRECTOR

D1405351

By **Michael Willis** and **Michael Fass**

"The kind of book that every director will
want to have at their elbow in the boardroom

First published in Great Britain 2004
by
Industrial Christian Fellowship
St Martin-in-the-Fields
Trafalgar Square
London, WC2N 4JJ

British Library in Cataloguing in Publications Data
A CIP catalogue record for this book is available from the British Library

ISBN 0-900487-01-1

Cover design by Vivid Images, London & Milan
Book typeset & printed by MD Print & Design, Edinburgh

Contents

ACKNOWLEDGEMENTS

The authors and publishers wish to acknowledge the debt owed to the Institute of Directors in the preparation of this book. The IoD is one of the world's premier business membership organisations and has become a well respected brand in leadership and direction. Because of our involvement with its members we have had the opportunity to work with many directors who have helped to shape and influence our thinking. We are grateful to our families, friends and colleagues for the encouragement they have given to us whilst writing the book and to the Industrial Christian Fellowship who have sponsored its production.

ABOUT THE AUTHORS

Michael Willis is an Economist and adviser to a wide range of organizations. He is a tutor for the IOD and for the last 8 years has run their 'flag-ship' course 'The Role of the Company Director and the Board' which over 300 Scottish directors have successfully completed - the only one of its type in Scotland. He is a founder member of Beyond Delancey Street Associates - a company specializing in board and director development as well as providing individual coaching.

He is Chairman of Falkirk Enterprise Action Trust and of a public-private property company which provides start-up and fast track incubator units for small businesses. He was formerly the CEO of a global supplier of electronic components and has spent 25 years in a variety of management and directorial roles. He was also a lecturer at the Universities of Durham and Stirling where he published a number of books and articles on international marketing.

Michael Fass manages the Institute of Directors director training operation in Scotland. He spent the first 17 years of his career in industry and commerce with the Hays Group, Miles-Druce GKN and Tricentrol and 18 years working for local and national government in the UK and Europe in the field of community based economic development during which he led one of the country's largest development agencies.

Michael has experience of being a CEO, non-executive director and chairman in limited companies and in not-for-profit and charitable organisations. He was a founder director of The Prince's Scottish Youth Business Trust, co-founder of Tomorrow's Company in Scotland and is the current Chairman of the Industrial Christian Fellowship (ICF), an ecumenical, UK-wide charity that supports Christians at work. In addition to managing director development programmes for over 350 delegates each year, he also shares the responsibility for the work of the IoD's Corporate Governance Unit in Scotland.

HOW TO USE THIS BOOK

The purpose of this book is to provide a practical guide to corporate governance for directors and others who are associated with the work of incorporated bodies. These may be aspiring, newly appointed or experienced directors and other individuals who, whilst not directly involved in governance themselves, need to understand the way companies work in order to fulfill their own responsibilities. The layout of the book is therefore designed to break down barriers between theory and practice and to make plain to everyone the way directors should govern their organisations.

The book is about finding ways for directors to renew their roles and is therefore always 'action orientated' because the authors want both individual directors and whole boards to work better. Each chapter encourages readers to reflect upon their own role as a director and to draw upon their own knowledge and experience to identify practical ways to implement the proposals that are outlined. The overall aim of the book is to encourage readers to take up the role of a faithful governor that will go beyond the simple fact of their directorial status or function.

After introducing the key themes of the book and some of the current issues in corporate governance, the authors describe the way that limited companies have developed and the different forms they have taken. One important theme that is fully explored is that of the trust that investors, shareholders and other stakeholders place in directors and the ways that this trust can be eroded as well as highlighting the opportunity for faithful service that the role implies.

A model of the director as a 'good steward' is created and is developed by examining issues such as the power, authority and leadership that is assumed to be part of the director's role. A recurring theme of the book is that of the faithfulness that is expected of directors with its long history: Understanding more about this can help directors to find new ways to act faithfully today.

Finally, some new ideas about the way that boards of directors can become excellent are developed alongside some helpful hints designed to keep directors out of trouble!

Each chapter sets out key issues, develops new ideas and concludes with a summary of learning and action points. Case studies are used to illustrate particular issues and there are a number of personal and corporate assessments, toolkits and exercises that readers can complete in order that they can assess the progress that they and their board are making towards becoming excellent governors.

Whilst the book is not about enterprise or entrepreneurialism as such, there is an obvious connection between the practice of good governance and the development of innovative governors who will also be those who are most likely to build successful companies. Good corporate governance can be an innovative activity in itself as well as being a way to introduce change into the company.

Governance is a fast moving area of research, of legislative change and of revised codes of best practice. Company Law is currently under review and directors are encouraged to keep up to date. For this reason a full list of useful addresses and web sites is included at the end of the book. In addition, readers are encouraged to post any of their comments, questions, reviews, or reflections onto the authors' web site at *www.faithingovernance.com.*

INTRODUCTION

"The health of the board is only as strong as the overall health of society"

A calling

It would be impossible to be a director of a limited company or trustee of a charitable organisation and not to be affected by the screaming headlines that have appeared daily in the news in the past two years or so about one director or board scandal or another. The behaviour and performance of directors has become a matter of the highest public policy with its attendant risk of interference by the State and is of interest to all those who are affected by the decisions directors take - be they responsible for large public companies or small community charities. The spotlight is well and truly on directors!

There are a number of reasons that this has happened. There is general cynicism about the quality of governance in both the public and private sectors, much of it driven by the media. There have been too many genuine scandals involving directors who have failed in their duty and there is a continuing debate about the need for more regulation. This book seeks to promote the role of the director as an honourable vocation and to help directors to renew their commitment to good stewardship. Society needs individuals who will work diligently as good stewards to carry out many of its functions. Good stewards produce good results and more successful companies produce more wealth, employment and tax revenues.

Trusting directors that they will act in good faith - which lies at the heart of the concept of 'fiduciary' duty - is the basis for the formation of every company, its subsequent activity and the work of its directors. This matters to everyone in society: Investors and shareholders, the users and consumers of products and services in both the public and private sectors and for all those who work in these organisations. Directors have enormous influence for good or ill and it is vital that they appreciate their roles and the difference they can make for the better.

Faith in the processes of governance - and in those who carry on its work - needs therefore to be continually renewed if this trust is to be sustained. Likewise, the ideas that lie behind it, that include assurance, confidence, reliability and loyalty, need to be fully explored and understood by directors.

This book proposes three leading themes for the development of excellence in governance and of faithful governors:

- That being a director is a profession and vocation which needs to be learned. This learning is about reflecting upon the roles and responsibilities that go along with the title and its functions and to develop not only the skills needed for the job but also the ability to change and adapt as circumstances alter - as they always will. To be an excellent governor means being also a learner and educator.

- That being a director is about being a good steward of what is usually other people's property; being trusted and being faithful to the objects of the company. This good stewardship needs application and understanding and it too has to be experienced and practised continually.

- That individual directors and the board of which he or she is a member have the **responsibility** for the future prosperity of the company, for the relationships the company should have with its stakeholders and, through its work, the contribution it can make to the overall health of society. This is a high calling.

These three themes represent the key aspects of being a director - and of being a faithful governor - and will recur throughout this book.

Being a director is more than making a profit; more than complying with governance rules and more than conformity to the latest regulatory fad. Individuals who are directors play a vital role in creating and sustaining the sort of society we want: Directors are called to act justly, provide leadership and to fulfil duty.

The authors believe that being a director is a worthy calling that requires much dedication, reflection, learning and practice and wish this book to contribute to this process.

The lessons of experience

Directors are a very diverse group. There are newly inducted directors in smaller concerns, experienced main board directors of listed corporations, directors of private, family-owned companies and directors of not for-profit organisations and trusts. Whatever their age or stage of development they all wish to play their part within the complex dynamic of the board room and to know more about the scope of their authority, their duties, the limitations placed on them by law and the penalties they might face due to failure or misconduct. Many wish to become more professional in their role and develop themselves although only c. 8% of appointed directors undertake some kind of formal training and development.

There are a number of important issues about the development of good governors that include:

- High performance in management does not necessarily equip individuals to perform well in the boardroom and managers need to develop themselves further to become excellent directors and governors. Being a director requires wisdom, judgement, integrity and an ability to ensure that the company will be governed using principles of natural justice and the common good.

- The real test of a director is how he or she performs and interacts with others on the board and uses their experience to reflect upon their current practise in association with the contributions of their colleagues

- It is the attitudes, attributes and tools of corporate governance that directors need to sharpen in the crucible that is the boardroom

- There is a long and distinguished tradition in corporate culture of probity within the boardroom - it is each director's responsibility to nurture these standards and to pass them on to future generations.

- Any framework for the practice of good governance should always be aimed at helping rather than hindering 'wealth creation' processes.

The vocation of a director calls him or her not only to serve in their own companies but also in other organisations which will benefit their community and society as a whole. This is another significant opportunity for the learning and professional development of directors which is of value to others.

Finally, directors, like any other individuals, will experience and struggle with corporate dilemmas which can often place the 'ways of the world' in tension with civilising principles of honesty, truthfulness and openness. Understanding the reasons for these tensions and the way that directors can respond to them can transform the practice of governance.

A passion for good governance

It falls particularly to the directors of companies and organisations to provide the leadership, inspiration and support needed by every individual who wishes fully to enter into the challenges that work offers. Work can never be 'humdrum' when creativity is at its centre and when directors are in the company of individuals dedicated to meeting common goals. Much of the quality of people's working lives is shaped by what happens in the boardroom and the more light that is shed upon its processes the more individual directors can be aware and better prepared for the immense responsibilities they have - and the opportunities they are given - to create the right conditions for sustainable success.

An emerging consensus

It has been said that a career in a for-profit business or not-for-profit community service organisation is unchallenging intellectually compared to life in the 'professions' as a doctor or teacher and there has been an historic aversion to hands-on involvement in the nitty-gritty of company and organisational life. This has done our society much harm over the generations and has placed us historically low in the league of successful and highly productive nations.

However, the lines between private and public have become increasingly blurred in the past 20 years as private sector companies have needed to be much more sensitive to their customers' needs - and their response to the public's perception of them - sometimes known as their 'Licence to Operate'. Successive governments, of all political persuasions, have also sought to dismantle large organisations in the public sector through privatisation, for example, British Airways and British Gas or to convert them into agencies, for example, the Passport Office and the DVLA, so that these are closer and more responsive to their users' needs.

Both private sector companies and public sector and community-based organisations have come, therefore, to share much of the same agenda and nowhere is this more apparent than in the area of what has come to be known as 'corporate governance'.

Why governance matters

Recently - and accelerated by the publicity given to such corporate disasters as the crash of the stock market's Dot.com favourites, the Enron affair, Marconi, a series of charity scams and the Bristol Infirmary scandal - there has been much attention upon those who govern and how they do it. Everyone is at some time in their life an investor, customer and even a victim of, corporate incompetence in private and public boardrooms that can often appear to be more about greed and self-interest than with constructive relationships with others. It can seem that whenever a light is shone inside boardrooms it reveals some apparent scandal and examples of the worst excesses of capitalism in the private sector or self-serving interests in the public.

This is profoundly unfair to directors, the great majority of whom seek to undertake their duties in an honest and truthful fashion. They are helped - although they may not fully appreciate it - by the fact that many of the principles surrounding and underpinning the governance of corporate organisations, and how directors should behave, have roots in historic ideas about faithfulness. These roots once uncovered can be used for the benefit of renewing the role of the director and to develop even more excellence in governance.

Only connect!

The Victorians who first tackled the framing of the early laws relating to companies understood the connection with faith as easily as they breathed the air. Whilst the pursuit of profit led some of them to treat their workforce with extreme indifference, it was nevertheless understood that there were limits to the scope of personal ambition and that human dignity should be respected. The great reformers of that era, for example, Robert Owen, the Fry family and Lord Shaftesbury demonstrated this search for excellence as they campaigned for better conditions at work.

However, the modern director, try as he or she might, finds it increasingly difficult to maintain these connections with the origins of good governance and many directors have lost the link entirely. The danger of this loss of collective memory is that if directors make up their own governance rules as they go along - literally anything goes!

The brilliant concept that became the limited liability company, was a privilege in return for which directors were expected to act as stewards on behalf of, and towards, the owners of the corporation who, it was clearly understood, would ultimately call them to account. Directors can never, therefore, serve only their own interests because at the heart of the principle of good governance lies the fiduciary duty of directors to act always in good faith and in the best interests of the company. This is a solemn and binding duty with as many consequences as those that are taken on, for example, in any faithful human relationship.

The concept of duty

Regrettably, all too many directors are completely oblivious of this corporate legal duty or choose, in some cases, to ignore its implications. An understanding of the concept of fiduciary duties and the wider responsibility to society that arises from being a director can help all directors to become better directors. They can then find more ways to cope with the day to day corporate dilemmas which they face and redress the apparent imbalance between some aspects of current corporate culture, which appears to have forgotten its origins in faithfulness, and one which places such faithful behaviour at its very centre.

This is an onerous task because, through work, humankind must earn its daily bread, and the director or trustee has many mouths to feed. Much is expected of him or her from shareholders, employees, colleagues, creditors and the local community and much needs to be learned and mastered.

Faith in governance

The words 'faith', 'faith in' and 'faithfulness have a number of different meanings. First, there is the 'fiduciary' duty owed by all directors to the company to which they are appointed; this has a particular meaning in the Companies Acts and is used throughout the book when describing the duties of directors working to these Acts and the Codes of Conduct which accompany them. Second, faith and faithfulness are concepts that are understood to have meaning in contemporary culture and affect the way individuals will understand their own role and the roles of others in a purely secular sense. This meaning is used in the book to explore issues of human behaviour and personal motivation. Third, 'faith in' can mean faith in a religious sense usually associated with a religious tradition or movement. This third meaning is used to provide both examples from history which have influenced present thinking and action about governance and models of power, authority and leadership upon which the reader can reflect.

Because some of the key meanings of these words come to us from the rich history and culture of the Judeo-Christian tradition, it is not possible to tell the story of governance, or to reflect upon its principles, without reference to them. It was from such traditions that the original 'map' of governance was first drawn. Whilst they may be considered by some to be outmoded, the model that was used to build the foundations of current governance practice is still understood as 'religious'. That is, it relied upon stories and standards set originally in the Bible. For example, the stories of prophets, princes and priests were the currency by which people compared their daily lives to their forebears and were the common measure which they used to indicate the quality of their individual and corporate relationships with what they thought of as the ideal.

To understand these origins is only one way to get back to the basics of good governance and to view faith in governance through any kind of religious lens, is only one way to do it. Throughout the book the role of a director-governor is affirmed as an historic and honourable one that, whilst requiring an appreciation of the word faith as used in the Companies Acts and in contemporary culture, does not require the exercise of any specifically religious faith. Wherever the language of faith is used, it is done for illustrative purposes in both its secular and religious meanings.

Conclusion

In the last few years a large literature has grown up around behaviour in the boardroom - and this field of research is called corporate governance. As the name suggests, it is concerned with the way corporate entities are governed, as distinct from how the day-to-day business within these companies and organisations is managed. Much of the literature associated with it is legalistic, over complex, and designed to be applied to large Stock-Exchange listed companies only. Too often it is of little practicable value to the busy practitioner in a smaller business, a not for-profit organisation or a charitable NGO.

In this book all types of corporate bodies - the family-owned company, the company limited by guarantee - often a charity or community owned and based initiative - the public listed company, the joint venture company and the wholly owned subsidiary company are all covered. Its contents are also relevant to the governance of charities, NDPBs, NGOs and not-for-profit companies and organisations in which directors are often referred to as 'Trustees'.

Its main focus is on the boards of companies and their directors or trustees who wish to govern their company or organisation on sound principles of good governance and these can be found to have their origins in traditions of faithfulness. Each chapter concludes with a practical summary of key points, case study material and further reading for reflection and discussion.

The whistleblower who first raised concerns about how Enron was being managed said that boardroom salaries and self-serving boards of directors were distorting the "moral compass" of individuals; that they had lost their way and that they no longer had that sense of right and wrong that lies at the heart of faithful action.

This book seeks to put that compass back into the boardroom and can be used as a practical guide to the behaviour, procedures and processes that should be expected at regular meetings of directors or trustees: The kind of handbook that every wise chairman or woman will have at his or her elbow! It is intended to help, to educate, to inform and to renew the role of the director so that he or she is transformed into an excellent governor!

CHAPTER ONE - ISSUES IN CORPORATE GOVERNANCE

- The field of research into corporate governance has grown in the wake of the corporate failures and public excesses of the 1980's and 1990's - although corporate failure and excess is nothing new

- Corporate governance is the system by which these incorporated companies and Trusts ought to be controlled and directed

- At the heart of the governance system is the concept of accountability to others, which is similar to a journey in which accountability before God is our ultimate destination

- Governing is not the same as running or managing an organization - it requires a completely different set of skills and often the wisdom of Solomon!

- One aspect of the corporate governance story is the continuing struggle to regulate corporations from the outside, often in opposition to them

The term 'corporate governance' is often used but less often understood. At its simplest it can be defined as the way that all corporations are governed. But why does this matter? It is a truism to say that if organisations are not effectively ruled they will end up being ill served by their own self-perpetuating history and structures and that this will lead inevitably to their atrophy and decline. This warning goes to the heart of the corporate governance debate: Without effective corporate governance, directors can end up pursuing competing, contrary and conflicting aims; sometimes acting illegally or immorally; or end up serving their own or other vested interests and losing sight of their overriding role which is to act always in the best interests of the company.

Alasdair Ross Gobey, one of the earliest investment managers in the City of London to take an interest in corporate governance, and CEO of Hermes Investment Trust which was formed originally to serve the investments needs of the Post office Pensions Fund, summed this up in his 'Hermes principle' which was that: 'Companies should be run in the long-term interests of their shareholders'. For some shareholders this principle will mean long-term increases in share value, for others a regular flow of dividends and for others a mix of the two. All the evidence suggests that without effective governance this is less likely to be achieved.

The scandal of corporations

Corporate scandal and the illegality and immorality which lies behind it is not new: For example, the collapse of the Mississippi Company (founded by Scotsman, John Law in France) and of the South Sea Company (founded by John Blunt, the son of a Baptist shoemaker in 1720 in London), almost destroyed the entire French and British economic and financial systems through greed, speculation and lies. The slave trading merchants of Bristol, Liverpool and London in the Eighteenth and the directors of companies in war- torn Europe in the Twentieth centuries, who commandeered slave labour to reduce operating costs, are also examples of directors who behaved without regard for human decency or conscience. Understandably whenever there is a whiff of corporate wrongdoing, the state calls for regulation.

Self-government v regulation

"There are too many 'great' men in the world: Legislators, organizers, do-gooders, leaders of the people, fathers of nations, and so on. Too many persons place themselves above mankind; they make a career out of organizing it, patronizing it, and ruling it." (**Bastiat**)

"If it moves tax it; if it keeps moving regulate it; if it stops moving subsidise it" (**Reagan, R.** the late President Reagan on the role of the Democratic government in supporting business).

An important issue for governance is the extent to which regulation helps or hinders the development of good governance. If there is too much, then there is a danger that those in governance forget their duty of faithfulness and become uninterested in it because the regulatory authorities will do it for them. Regulation will not necessarily produce the high performing boards of tomorrow. Conformance to regulation creates the 'box ticking' mentality that has crippled the productivity of our boards. Conformance is only the beginning of a much more exciting journey towards even more enterprising styles of governance. Insufficient regulation on the other hand may provide a regulatory framework that is so slack as to positively encourage wrong doing. Statism and regulation can create an unhealthy reliance on government structures to solve social and moral problems. Government and its array of powers can end up being charged with solving social, economic and moral problems for which it has no expertise or resources. This trust in Government to solve every problem in corporations can lead to frantic activity that disrupts the boards of companies and undermines society's willingness and ability to regulate itself.

In general, the free market resists regulation claiming that it distorts market mechanisms and adds unnecessary cost to any free market economic system. The drive for the introduction of Codes of Conduct which prescribe board behaviour, and other governance guidance introduced by the private sector, reflects the desire of those who direct corporations to regulate themselves so as to ensure their own sound corporate governance rather than to provoke intervention by the state.

However, the public appears unconvinced and remains suspicious and distrustful about what goes on behind the closed doors of the boardroom so that the clamour for regulation is likely to increase if and when further examples of corporate failure come to light. But as Neil Collins has remarked: *"As the burdens are piled on, our enthusiastic legislators, regulators and pressure groups should remember that the ultimate purpose of a company is to make profits. If it fails to do that, it collapses, leaving no jobs, frustrated customers and no taxes to sustain those legislators, regulators and pressure groups"* (**Daily Telegraph**). Fred Goodwin, the CEO of the Royal Bank of Scotland, made this same point more forcefully when he defended the largest ever UK bank profits of £7.15 billion against accusations of profiteering at the expense of customers when he remarked: *"56% of profits go back to shareholders in the form of dividends, 13% is retained profit and is reinvested in the business, while some 31% goes to the Treasury in taxes to help fund the government's public service spending programme...maybe if there were more companies like us, bonus payments from with-profits insurance policies wouldn't be going down."* (**The Herald**)

Corporate governance: A definition

The Cadbury Code (1992) - the first of a long series of reports and codes on corporate governance that have promoted self-regulation - defined Corporate Governance as: 'The system by which companies are directed and controlled.' Thus corporate governance should be consistent and systematic rather than vague and sporadic and governance should be about 'directing' and 'controlling' the organization rather than 'organizing' and 'managing' it. The board of directors is responsible for the governance of a company. This responsibility was described by the late Lord Denning in the following way:

"A company may in many ways be likened to a human body. It has a brain and nerve centre which controls what it does. It also has hands which hold the tools and act in accordance with directions from the centre. Some of the people in the company are mere servants and agents who are nothing more

than hands to do the work and cannot be said to represent the mind or will. Others are directors and managers who represent the directing mind and will of the company and control what it does. The state of mind of these managers is the state of mind of the company and is treated as such by the law." (**Denning**)

Smaller companies and trusts

"But what has all this got to do with me!" is often the response of a director or owner of a smaller business, Charity or Trust: and, "Why can't I go on managing the business the way I've always done?"

There are 6 main drivers for change -

• A company is a distinct legal entity and under Company Law, other related Parliamentary and legal regulation and the company's own Articles and Memorandum, the specific duties and responsibilities of directors are defined.

• Even though a director may be the 100% owner of the business, his or her prime duty is to act in the best interests of the company rather than himself or herself as the sole shareholder - more of this complex distinction later!

• A director's failure to grasp the distinction between managing and the legal duties of directing, can result in severe penalties under the law as ignorance is not deemed to be a sufficient excuse! In the same way, trustees of charities are personally liable for any losses caused by breaches of trust on their part.

• As a part of the story of the way businesses go through their lifecycles of start-up, growth, maturity and succession, there will always come a time in the development and growth of, particularly, every family-owned business when the issues of good corporate governance will need to be addressed.

• Although adherence to codes of corporate governance conduct are not yet enforceable for smaller, unlisted companies, they can provide a very helpful support structure for companies as they grow and expand - particularly in the way boards are composed and new directors appointed and remunerated. Outside investors will often seek assurances about the independence of directors and the way the board works before they are willing to invest.

- There is very strong evidence to suggest that well governed boards can lead to prosperous, vibrant and successful companies
- It is expected that Trustees upon appointment bring with them a good understanding of governance

Models of good governance

The key elements of governance are easy to map but more difficult to implement.

Figure1.1 depicts the essentials of corporate governance which we term the 'focused' model. The three main participants are the shareholders of the company, the board of directors and the management of the company (some of whom will also be executive directors and some directors can also be shareholders). At the very least ordinary shareholders have the right to securely register and if need be transfer their shares; obtain timely information about the company's performance; participate and vote in shareholder meetings; elect members of the board and most importantly share in the profits of the organization. The prime governing role of the board is to ensure accountability to the shareholders by generating profits and long term shareholder value. To do this they should exercise their delegated powers from shareholders to control management and ensure these managers are accountable to the board; in addition they should provide direction to the business to protect the interests of the shareholders and generate long-term value.

Accountability, transparency & prudence

Accountability can be defined as: "A formal duty to disclose what you have done" and although the Annual General Meeting (AGM) is the time when this duty to disclose is formally exercised, throughout the year the actions of a well run board will always consider the best interests of the owners of the company or sponsors of the organisation. This continual state of preparedness is in tune with one of the key principles of faithfulness which is to be always vigilant and accountable to others. Under UK law, shareholders have the power to change the board at virtually any time and for any reason. 10% of shareholders can call an Extraordinary General Meeting ("EGM") for any purpose and 50% of those shareholders present at such meeting can replace any or all of the company directors.

One guiding principle in preparation of being called to account is prudence, defined by the best known medieval thinker Thomas Aquinas as: "Right reason in action". Unfortunately prudence, recently a much loved virtue of politicians, has in ordinary speech, acquired a meaning which is entirely contradictory when it implies 'playing safe', being 'risk averse' and having a 'steady pair of hands'. In fact, prudence is the virtue which helps us to form the 'right' judgement before taking action and which can be highly innovative and risky. Knowledge and experience are also important elements in forming the ability to make prudent judgements.

Corporate governance cannot function without transparency and this requires the unfettered exchange of information between the company owners, its board and the management. One Christian writer commenting upon transparency wrote: 'There is nothing hidden that will not be disclosed, nor anything concealed that will not be known'. (**Luke Ch. 8v17**). Wise advice for the corporate governor!

The focused model

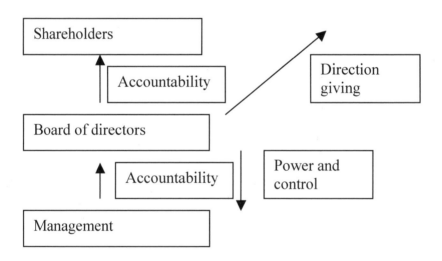

figure 1.1 The 'focused' Corporate Governance Model

Expanding the governance agenda

The OECD later amplified the Cadbury definition: "Corporate governance is the system by which business corporations are directed and controlled. The corporate governance structure specifies the distribution of rights and responsibilities among different participants in the corporation, such as, the board, managers, shareholders and other stakeholders, and spells out the rules and procedures for making decisions on corporate affairs. By doing this, it also provides the structure through which the company objectives are set, and the means of attaining those objectives and monitoring performance."(OECD)

This definition takes into account the additional roles of 'stakeholders' as well as shareholders in the definition of corporate governance. This we have termed the 'diffused' model of governance - also widely known as the 'Stakeholder' model of corporate governance.

The diffused model

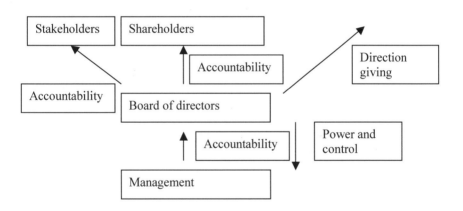

figure 1.2 The 'diffused' Corporate Governance Model

Whilst the 'focused'-shareholder model of governance advocates the overriding concern of directors to be accountable to shareholders, as they are the owners of the shares in the company and thus enjoy property rights; the 'diffused'- stakeholder model asserts that corporations need to earn their 'licence to operate' from society and the community in which they are set because of wider societal expectations and concerns.

Stakeholder expectations arise from within such groups as customers, employees, suppliers and the local community and it is in partnership with such stakeholders that the company is expected to assume its societal role and meet community objectives by embracing what is now known as 'Corporate Social Responsibility' (CSR). Many corporations now pursue a 'triple bottom line'- accounting for economic, social and environmental results and outcomes rather than profits and shareholder value only.

Confusion can arise between these two approaches: "Some commentators take too narrow a view, and say it (corporate governance) is the fancy term for the way in which directors and auditors handle their responsibilities towards shareholders. Others use the expression as if it were synonymous with shareholder democracy. Corporate governance is a topic recently conceived, as yet ill-defined, and consequently blurred at the edges...corporate governance is a subject, an objective, or a regime to be followed for the good of shareholders, employees, customers, bankers and indeed for the reputation and standing of our nation and its economy" (**Maw et al.**)

J. Wolfensohn, president of the World Bank concentrated his definition on outputs and broadened the definition of corporate governance when he was quoted as saying that: "Corporate governance is about promoting corporate fairness, transparency and accountability"(**Financial Times**). However, this begs the question: What is 'corporate fairness?' Does it include fairness in all business dealings, employment matters and relations with consumers? Does it include fairness in the distribution of profits and dealings with the local community and environmental issues? These are difficult questions upon which boards will need to have clear views.

The global context for corporate governance

In their 'Principles of corporate governance' the OECD has provided a helpful analysis of corporate governance -

"The corporate governance structure specifies the distribution of rights and responsibilities among different participants in the corporation, such as, the board, managers, shareholders and other stakeholders, and spells out the rules

and procedures for making decisions on corporate affairs. By doing this, it also provides the structure through which the company objectives are set, and the means of attaining those objectives and monitoring performance."

And more importantly explores the reasons that good governance is critical within a global context:

"Good corporate governance is an important step in building market confidence and encouraging more stable, long-term international investment flows. The business-corporation is an increasingly important engine for wealth creation worldwide, and how companies are run will influence welfare in society as a whole. In order to serve this wealth creating function, companies must operate within a framework that keeps them focused on their objectives and accountable for their actions. That is to say, they need to establish adequate and credible corporate governance arrangements. Many countries see better corporate governance practices as a way to improve economic dynamism and thus enhance overall economic performance. The importance of good corporate governance has also been highlighted by the recent turbulence in financial markets." (**OECD**)

Governance v management

What is clear is that governance has little to do with management although this often comes as a surprise to directors. It is not a hands-on activity that can be learned then put into action easily. It is a whole-board activity and not something that can be delegated to the company secretary or the chairperson only. Whilst it will always be helpful to consider the views of a number of commentators and of the issues arising within the current governance debate, the real location for the creation of good governance is the boardroom and within each and every board member who is on it.

Whilst management operates within a hierarchy of delegated responsibility and authority, the members of a board are all are jointly and individually responsible with equal rights and duties. Bob Tricker, a well known commentator on governance, depicts the board as a circle superimposed on the pyramid of hierarchical management (see Figure1.3) (**Tricker,R.**). The board is concerned with governance and the management organization with managing. Some of the senior management at the top of the hierarchy will also sit on the board. This is the reason the system of governance in the United Kingdom is called the 'unitary' board system rather than the European, 'two-tier' board system or 'supervisory' board where the board is completely separate from the management hierarchy.

Governance v management

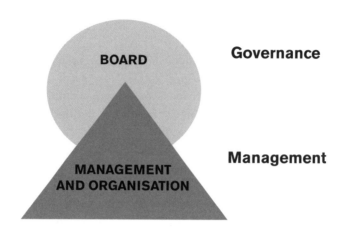

figure 1.3 The distinction between management and governance

Many directors fail to make this important connection: They have been promoted to the board on the basis of their skills and success in managing and getting things done and find the more intellectual, collegial and conceptual nature of governance an irritation and barrier to full participation and achieving excellence.

The family firm and governance

Although there can be confusion in family owned companies when there is insufficient separation between managing and governance, such companies are often an ideal place to learn the practice of good governance. Unfortunately, much of the current literature on governance lacks relevance to the family company because of its over legalistic language and obscure approach. However, as these family companies expand and their ownership becomes more diffused with second and third generation family members and shareholders working both inside and outside the company, it becomes more urgent to govern clearly so as to ensure that policy and strategy issues are not submerged by family issues. Sir Adrian Cadbury quotes the case of a vegetable garden causing major ructions within a family-owned company!

"I was once involved in a dispute in a family firm over the produce from a vegetable garden. The family home, factory and garden were all on the same site and the garden was cultivated for the benefit of those members of the family who lived on the spot. When this apparently modest benefit came to be costed out, it was clear that it was a totally uneconomic way of keeping some members of the family in fresh vegetables, quite apart from the development value of the land tied up in food production. Any change in the traditional arrangement was, however, seen by those who benefited from it as an attack on the established order and the beginning and the end of the family firm. Eventually, the fate of the vegetable plot was satisfactorily settled." (**Sir Adrian Cadbury**)

When family owned companies are able to regulate the relationships they have between company and family by separating management from governance, they are able to move away from day to day issues and 'head-off' potential squabbles. Whilst the family and the company may in reality be the same, making the distinction can be helpful when non-family directors are to be appointed, a successor to the founder is to be agreed or when the company seeks to raise external finance. The following case illustrates these points.

Case Study - Bitesize Electronics

Jim Case is the founder and principal owner of Bitesize electronics - specializing in the miniaturizing of computer peripherals and networking products. The business has expanded rapidly to £25m turnover after 3 years under Jim's stewardship as chairman and CEO. To assist in the financing of future growth and expansion into European markets he has bought in a venture capital company - Buzzard Finance. They have 29% of the shareholding and a nominee director - Richard Starling - representing their interests on the board. Jim has a team of 3 competent executive directors - Helen Jarvis Marketing, Keith Robson Technical and Richard Case, the son of the founder, who has a CIMA qualification and covers the finance function. Richard has 8% of the equity and Richard Starling is insisting that the other directors are offered share options but Jim is resisting this. The final place on the board is taken up by Ronald van Buuren - a brother-in-law of Jim who helped provide some finance at start-up - and he has 10% of the equity. Jim dominates the company and the board; his judgement of commercial opportunities has been spot on but he is beginning to resent the interference of Richard Starling who is insisting on more formal board meetings and a debate about the expansion into Europe as well as pushing the share options issue. Both Helen and Keith are adamant that Bitesize should concentrate on their UK customers and not over extend the company.

As part of Jim's development plans for Europe he has entered into an informal agreement with a Dutch distributor. This was done just before Buzzard Finance came on board and was not declared as part of the Investment Agreement and was certainly not part of any board discussion. The distributor has since bought a claim against the company for failing to supply goods on time. The situation is getting nasty. Jim turns to his trusted friend Ronald. What advice should Ronald give?

Discussion points:

- Should the roles of CEO and chairman be separated?

- What are the problems which arise when executive powers are concentrated?

- How balanced is the board of Bitesize?

- Is information about the company's activities supplied in a timely manner which enables the board to discharge its duties?

- How should a board deal with minority shareholders?

- What exactly is a 'nominee' director and how different are their duties and responsibilities to those of an executive director?

- What does this case study imply about collective board responsibility?

- What are the implications in the case study for honesty and transparency?

Conclusion

There is an expanding and sometimes confusing literature about corporate governance. Most of it is aimed at the larger, global corporations and has been fuelled by distrust of the motives of the directors of these corporate giants: Do they operate for their own self-interest or do they act also in the interests of their owners and other stakeholders and do they believe that they need to be truly accountable for their actions? At the World Economic Forum in Davos in 2003, the theme of the Forum was 'building trust' following the Enron and Worldcom scandals. Already, in 2004, the apparent corporate irresponsibility at Parmalat, Equitable Life and Hollinger seems to suggest no light at the end of the tunnel.

Relations, both inside and beyond the corporation, are based on trust and as the current crisis in trust deepens, tinkering with corporate governance regulations feels like re-arranging the chairs on the Titanic. Good governance is a model of what should happen but there is a real battle taking place about where power should lie - with the shareholder-owners, the board of directors, the regulatory authorities or the influence of consumers.

The practice of governing is certainly different from managing: It is not about managing companies but ensuring they are well run. It is less about doing and taking action than reflecting and learning. One of its key principles, that of prudence, has already been commented upon and other ideas about governance will be explored such as acting in good faith, stewardship, duty, openness, transparency and integrity. These are the real building-blocks of excellence in corporate governance and the binding actions for an effective board.

CHAPTER TWO - THE COMPANY WE SERVE - ITS ORIGINS

"Did you ever expect a corporation to have a conscience, when it has no soul to be damned, and no body to be kicked!" (Thurlow 1781-1829)

- The word 'corporate' is rooted in the Latin 'corpus' - meaning a body. The word 'company' has its origins in the words 'com pane', the breaking of bread together and incorporated companies are considered to be 'distinct persons' in law

- Governance demands the virtue of service to an 'artificial' legal person. This should be considered as a calling or vocation

- Profit is legitimate and a good thing. Not only is it a universal way to indicate that a business is functioning well, but it is also the prime obligation of a corporate governor. In the not for-profit and charitable sectors, alternative, clear and easily indicated measures of performance will be needed.

- Corporations form an important component within a healthy and free society; they enjoy a rich tradition of which everyone should be reminded.

- Can the sense of purpose and 'missionary' zeal of the early corporations serve as a relevant model for directors today?

- Individuals are free to create corporations and serve the needs of others through mutually beneficial exchange. This is a privilege with enormous consequences.

Why it matters

Understanding the concept of the body corporate - or company - and how it has emerged is important for those who govern them. Why?

First, these institutions are not the post-modern constructs of a capitalist and materialistic age but enjoy a remarkable tradition and continuity that should be celebrated rather than ignored. The modern company, trust and charity are all the inheritors of a rich pattern of conventions, practice, law, and custom that are a part of society's inherited culture. For example, the books of the Bible are full of precepts and rules about the conduct of commerce and trade and it is made clear that organizations and individuals who act ethically will have their rewards and share in success.

Second, directors are the products of an age that is generally 'anti-institution'. Organisations such as the armed forces, the Monarchy, the family and the corporate body are questioned and society appears to have lost its respect for many institutions simply because they are established and have a pre-modern origin. One way to promote the positive role of good governance in contemporary culture is therefore to start reclaiming some of this lost ground and to celebrate governance's historic roots - which are also society's roots. To do this, directors need to act positively and to appreciate the value of their corporations and their roles at work because they perform key roles within both local communities and national economies.

In addition, directors should remember that the work they undertake within corporations forms a part of a key dimension of human existence and, in the light of recent hostility towards them, there is an urgent need to review corporations and the vocational nature of the work that goes on within them - particularly in relation to the role of directors as both their leaders and servants.

Lastly, if new and vital links can be made between some of the positive aspects of the corporation in contemporary culture, directors can find new ways to renew the spirit of duty and responsibility that all corporate leaders need if they are to be faithful. The alternative is that they run the risk of paying lip service to good governance by maintaining an outward resemblance of the standards expected of them but in reality serve our own interests alone. This latter approach could be summed up as: 'What is the minimum level of compliance with the law and various regulatory codes that I can get away with?'

Historical precedents

Since time immemorial individuals have formed associations to pursue common interests, share risks and accumulate wealth. It is worth reflecting on these traditions, some of which survive today, because they can teach us about the adaptive nature of corporations and their long-term contribution to the economic, spiritual and social welfare of their members and stakeholders. The Guilds or Livery companies are one such example and can trace their roots back to pre-Conquest times. Guilds or mysteries - from the Latin 'misterium', meaning 'professional skill' - thrived across Europe for many centuries and, amongst other activities, fixed wage rates and created supply monopolies. Until the Sixteenth century all work was undertaken in a moral context in which every action could bring people closer to or further away from judgement.

As opportunities emerged for opening up new markets many of the guilds invested in the Merchant Venturer Chartered Companies which sought exclusive rights of trade from the Crown for different overseas territories. The most famous of these was the East India Company whose power lasted into the mid 19th century. There was also the Russia Company, the Africa Company and the Levant Company, whilst the Virginia Company was responsible for much of the early settlement and investment in the State of Virginia.

Many of these organizations transformed themselves to become vehicles for imperialist government and military strength. Universities and towns formed chartered companies in the Middle Ages and Aberdeen Harbour Board established in 1136 is perhaps the world's oldest commercial company. Some thirty Harbour Authorities continue to operate under statutory powers for the purpose of improving, maintaining or managing a harbour and take great pride in their ancient lineage. Whilst companies such as the East India Company provided some opportunities for investors to take up a share in its ownership, the South Sea Bubble scandal of 1720 blighted the reputation of the joint-stock companies and as a consequence the Crown and Government tightly regulated the formation and longevity of this type of corporation.

The legal position of charities can be traced back to the 1601 Statute of Elizabeth when charitable purposes were defined as the relief of poverty, the advancement of education and religion and for other purposes of benefit to the community.

An even earlier example of the power and influence of the corporation in Europe and one from which lessons can still be learned, was the tradition of the great monasteries. The one built by Benedict in 529AD rose 1600 feet on an almost sheer peak above the town of Cassino in Italy - a formidable site for a corporate HQ and some of the corporate barons of today would envy the ability of St Benedict to mould his people around a clearly understood and universally accepted Mission Statement! He persuaded them to live out his guiding principles and ethics in their daily work and prayer life - as they do to this day - all clothed in the same corporate uniform!

In addition they were able to be fully self-sufficient in goods and services and dispense with the need for an extensive supply chain. In an era of poor transport links and no access to the mass media, they undertook a massive round of overseas investment which enabled them to franchise - a Norman word for privilege - their corporate brand throughout the known world.

The soul-less corporation

Much of the language constructed around the concept of the company and the corporation can be negative and demeaning. Companies are 'liquidated'; their assets are 'stripped'. Like a can of peas, we can buy 'shell' companies 'off the shelf'; put them 'off-shore', sell them to the 'highest bidder' and then 'write them off' like an unwanted pet. The corporation is termed as 'faceless' and 'soulless'.

Most of those who work in companies speak about them with derision - the majority of individuals would like to leave their employer and go to work elsewhere, given the opportunity. Often this can mean joining another corporation with yet another equally dissatisfying mission statement. Anti-capitalists view corporations as soul-less organisms destined to mutate globally and take over the free world. This has some resonance with the way that Thomas Hobbes (1588-1679) the great English thinker thought when he wrote in 'The Leviathan': "Corporations... are many lesser commonwealths in the bowels of a greater, like worms in the entrails of a natural man."

In post-modern language there appears to be an 'attitude' problem with the corporation. 'Corporate' man or woman is ridiculed; they have sold their soul to the corporation for the sake of material success and ranking in the hierarchy of the corporate 'jungle'. Is it in any wonder that society's attitudes about the concept of the company breeds public mistrust and disaffected workers!

As a result companies are much maligned and corporate governors need to renew their roles to perform even more effectively and to project a more positive image of the company and the contribution they make to its success. It's not all gloom and doom and some writers exalt the company and contend that: "The most important organization in the world is the company...the company's only real rival for our time and energy is the one that is taken for granted - the family!"(**Micklethwait, J. & Wooldridge, A.**), and that companies are: "The basis of the prosperity of the West and the best hope for the future of the world".

"Gain all you can....save all you can....give all you can"

What then is the truth about corporations? There is some truth in both of the extreme statements shown above but the reality lies somewhere in between. Corporations are run by human beings who are frail and who will make mistakes. It would be foolish to damn corporations and the way they are governed on the basis of a few high profile cases of corporate greed and wrongdoing. One way to reach the truth about corporations, and society's attitude towards them, is to address that great shibboleth of corporate life - profit. Put simply, profits are the life-blood of the body corporate. Attack profits and the role of the corporation is threatened. Since the great majority of working age people and their families depend on corporations for their livelihoods (the Third Sector accounts for some 4.7% of employment and the public sector is financed by the corporation and income tax taken from those who work in the private sector), it is right that directors are concerned with sustaining the profitability of the corporations for which they are responsible.

The pursuit and maintenance of profit is therefore the first and prime obligation of a private corporation. Through the achievement of sustainable long-term profits both employees and other stakeholders are able to meet their own responsibilities to their families and others. Likewise, many not for-profit organizations seek to generate levels of surplus that can be placed into reserves as a contingency against future needs and to provide the capital needed to match with publicly provided funds. The famous preacher John Wesley once said: "Gain all you can...Save all you can...Give all you can" and this provides a helpful pointer for the corporate governor.

Case Study: Standard Life

In April 2003, the CEO of Standard Life, one of Europe's largest insurers and headquartered in Scotland, defended the bonuses paid to its directors and sparked off a row about 'Fat cats' and 'Rewards for failure'. The Scotsman's headline read: 'Unfairly treated' as the CEO attempted to defend the payments. "On the whole, you see, I don't agree that Standard Life has done incredibly badly. If the Remuneration Committee thinks it has done its job correctly, then it would be destructive to turn around and say 'I think you've done it all wrong and I'm going to forego something'". The CEO received a 26% increase in overall remuneration to £619,000 last year whilst Standard Life cut its payouts to policyholders by 15% and lost £4.7 billion on the stock market. One disgruntled policyholder began organising a campaign to de-mutualise the company which would then become a publicly quoted stock, completely changing its ownership structure. By January 2004 the CEO has departed and the company has been forced to consider a stock exchange listing as a way of raising capital and meeting the requirements of the FSA. In the meantime the value of the company has halved.

This case was about the application of equity; how individuals can become detached by their leadership positions from the world in which their stakeholders - in this example, their owners - live, and how the wisdom, that the exercise of right authority should bring, can fail. Whilst policy holders were receiving their 'treatment' by suffering the pain of greatly reduced incomes, the 'fat cats' saw no reason to show wage restraint; the judgment about whether the business had performed well or badly was internalised by the individual most closely involved and this same leader did not exercise his powers of leadership to override a self-serving decision made by a subordinate committee which he and his Board had themselves created. The episode damaged the reputation of the business and its leaders for sound judgment and equitable behaviour; faith in their governance faltered.

- How does your board make decisions on director remuneration?
- Are levels of remuneration sufficient to attract and retain directors?
- Is your policy formal and transparent?
- How does it fit with your policy on employee remuneration?

Why are corporations formed?

What exactly does it mean to incorporate? Put simply, incorporation allows a company of people to come together - or incorporate (from the Latin 'corparae', to make corporal, or physically embody) - and to pursue a particular economic or idealistic objective together.

Dave Packard, the co-founder of HP, in a speech to his employees in 1960 (**Collins & Porrus**) explained his reasoning for a company's formation: "I think many people assume, wrongly, that a company exists simply to make money. While this is an important result of a company's existence, we have to go deeper and find the real reasons for our being. As we investigate this, we inevitably come to the conclusion that a group of people get together - and exist as an institution that we call a company - so they are able to accomplish something collectively that they could not accomplish separately. They make a contribution to society, a phrase which sounds trite but is fundamental."

The community of persons

The present Pope, John Paul II combined the thoughts of David Packard with reflections on the pursuit of profits when he wrote: "In fact, the purpose of a business firm is not simply to make a profit, but is to be found in its very existence as a community of persons who in various ways are endeavouring to satisfy their basic needs, and who form a particular group at the service of the whole of society."(**John Paul II**)

It is easy to lose sight of this profound truth: that incorporated bodies are not soul-less just because they cannot be touched but that at their heart they are a community of persons which can be felt. In a democratic society, individuals should be as free as possible to join together in pursuit of lawful purposes and should expect minimal interference from the state. Without such freedoms it would be difficult to encourage individuals in the community to come forward and use their skills for the public benefit often on a voluntary basis. This applies particularly in the 'Third Sector' in which voluntary organisations play such a vital role in building social cohesion and inclusion and tackling local social and economic problems

Organisations develop into real communities of persons, strengthen the social fabric and prevent society from becoming anonymous and impersonal. It is in these inter-relationships on many levels that a person lives, and that society becomes more "personalized" and in which individuals can experience 'right relationship'.

The individual today can become trapped between the State and the marketplace. At times it can feel as if individuals are merely producers, consumers or providers of goods or are objects of State administration and sight is lost of the fact that the life of society has neither the market nor the State as its final purpose: It is life itself that has a unique value which both the State and the market serve.

Questions for corporate governors

•   What do you understand by the 'heritage' of your company?

•   What was the original intention of its founder members?

•   Is this intention still clearly understood by your colleagues?

•   When was the last time your board consulted its Memorandum and Articles of Association?

•   What do these documents tell you about how your company should be governed?

•   What language does your board use when describing the company? Is it in positive language or do you fall into the trap of deriding the company?

- Do you undertake your professional tasks to the highest standards and strive to attain the highest skills in your profession?

- Do you serve the company with an authentic desire and consider your role as a calling or vocation?

- What is your board's view on its sustainable level of long-term profitability?

- Does your board fully appreciate the moral imperative of achieving profitability?

Conclusion

The majority of us spend our working lives within incorporated bodies. The most fundamental questions we can ask ourselves are: Do we serve or are we enslaved? Do we serve the corporation diligently or do we serve ourselves? Profit-making is one consequence of incorporation - it is a legitimate and healthy activity within a free society. The development of the corporation is a core aspect of this society and has acted as a bulwark against the power of the State. The current - and sometimes hysterical - attacks on corporations could become an attack upon the freedoms and liberties they represent. The opportunity for individuals to freely associate and form a company without state interference is a precious right. The contemporary reliance on regulatory structures to solve social and moral problems can become unhealthy. 'Statism' can become the enemy of enterprise and a real threat to the freedom of the individual to create corporations and serve the needs of others through mutually beneficial exchanges. Good governors protect the integrity of the corporations in which they work and act as their servant-leaders exercising authority in their name. This is a high calling.

If we are not careful, the price of bad governance - or the suggestion of it - will be more and more regulation until the prospect of being a director will be so daunting that no one will be prepared to fulfill the role. Good governance of our corporations is a guardian of our freedom but it has to be continually learned and practised, reviewed and improved.

CHAPTER THREE - THE COMPANY
WE SERVE - ITS ROLE AND FORM

- The invention of the joint stock company separated ownership form management and was one of the great innovations of the C19th.

- The original idea of the incorporated company was to limit the liability of shareholder but the liability of directors remained unlimited

- The company is founded as an immortal body - this has profound implications for the way they are directed and nurtured.

- There are many natures and forms of corporate structure - placing different demands on those who govern.

- What lessons can be learned from the 'Third sector' which appears to offer more robust models of governance?

The Joint-Stock Company Act 1844

Until the passing of the Joint Stock Company Act in 1844, the idea of separating ownership from management appeared somewhat immoral to British culture as it was generally accepted that the owners would be the best trustees for the well-being of their own business. The risk of the Debtors jail and the Poor House provided a healthy incentive to select only low-risk business ventures and the powerful image of Mr Pickwick's eternal struggle with his creditors has no doubt dissuaded countless schoolchildren from entering into the world of commerce! Before the 1844 Act, the liability of the owners was unlimited and there was little incentive to invest in the high-risk sunrise industries of the burgeoning industrial revolution, such as the railways which were in desperate need of capital to support development and the expansion of overseas markets.

However, by the end of the 19th century the separation of ownership and management was the accepted standard - and the rest of the story is history! The 1844 Act, and its subsequent amendments, gave corporate status to a company and the legal capacity for it to act as an artificial 'person' as distinct from the natural human persons who held the capital and were its shareholders. Incorporation meant the company was an independent legal entity and with a separate legal life to the actual owners. The company became a legal person able to own its assets, buy and sell them, incur debts, employ people, sue and be sued and - most importantly - issue tradeable shares to any number of investor-shareholders and that these shareholders should have limited liability so that they would lose only the initial investment that they had committed to the company and would not be liable for its debts.

This was the unique and key device of the joint-stock company - the limitation of the liability of its original investors. It should be stressed that although the liability of shareholders was limited under the 1844 Act and all its subsequent modifications, the liability of directors remains unlimited to this day. This is the reason that ensuring the highest standards of corporate governance is of such significance.

An innovative model

Peter Drucker described the coming into being of these new style corporations - which were rapidly copied throughout Europe in Germany and France - as an innovation and not a reform: "It was the first autonomous institution in hundreds of years, the first to create a power centre that was within society yet independent of the central government of the national state."**(Drucker)** Mindful of the interests of creditors - those suppliers of goods and services to the company who no longer had recourse to the owners for bad debts - the legislators pushed through follow-up amendments which regulated the transparency of the accounting records of companies to enable these 'unsecured' creditors to assess the level of risk before releasing their goods and services to the company on credit.

The Companies Act of 1862 consolidated the inspired innovations of Gladstone's government which had passed the original Act of 1844 which has been regularly revised and modernised since then and with which we are familiar today.

Although a company became a person in law, it was clearly not a natural person. Human beings may be free to do anything they choose whilst it was legislated that a company:

- Can only act though its appointed agents - the board of directors

- Can only act in accordance with its constitutional documents agreed by the founding members at the moment of incorporation - its Memorandum and Articles of Association

The sense of immortality

Perhaps the most innovative concept about incorporated bodies that was introduced was that, unlike human persons, they are assumed to last longer than any individual who might from time to time be associated with them so that: "The act of incorporation implied a degree of 'immortality'. To survive and grow companies require a flow of profits and the ability to adapt and change to market and economic conditions. The implicit assumption about continuity is so strong that a company formed for a limited purpose - eg to work an exhaustible resource such as a single mine - will normally emphasise this unusual feature." **(IOD)**

"Companies have proved to be enormously powerful not just because they improve productivity, but also because they possess most of the legal rights of a human being, without the attendant disadvantages of biology: They are not condemned to die of old age and they can create progeny pretty much at will" (**Micklethwaite and Wooldridge**)

This feature of incorporation places a special duty on the directors of a company - they are not governing towards surviving next year's AGM, or even in the medium-term, they are governing for successive members and shareholders over many generations. This theme has been developed further: "When they - the individuals composing a corporation - are consolidated and unite into a corporation, they and their successors are considered as one person in law...for all the individual members that have existed from the foundation to the present time, or that shall ever hereafter exist, are but one person in law - a person that never dies; in the manner as the river Thames is still the same river, though the parts which compose it are changing every instant" (**Blackstone**)

Of course, many companies die very young - within 3 years 40% of all start-up companies cease to trade - and few are able to match the longevity of Aberdeen Harbour Board at 868 years. Those that do survive are often acquired by their larger or more successful competitors as the founding entrepreneurs run out of steam and are forced to sell. But this should not distract the diligent director from protecting and nurturing the company for long-term aims. There is a delicate balance to be maintained between preserving immortality on the one hand and taking risks to exploit change and opportunities for growth in the short term on the other. For the owner-director the idea of immortality should help them to develop the company's long-term rather than short-term self-interest. Directors should therefore be cultivators - they should develop future rootstock from which new generations can harvest the fruit.

Corporate variety

Incorporated companies are found within the public, private and charitable sector. They are not just a vehicle for 'raw' capitalism but their unique design provides protection for founding members across a wide spectrum of applications. These companies function within a legal framework of statute - principally the Companies Act 1985 - and the Common Law. Subject to these constraints, the company's activities are governed by its Memorandum and Articles of Association, often known as their 'M & As'. There are over 1.2 million companies incorporated with limited liability in the United Kingdom at present. Records in the 12 months to April 2004 show that 394,000 companies were incorporated during the period and this trend is likely to continue as the creation of a limited liability company remains a more tax efficient way to do business than to act as a sole trader. However, only 3,000 are Public limited companies that are listed on public stock exchanges so that any individual who chooses can invest in them.

Such giant corporations embrace around half of those in private sector employment. However, over 98% of incorporated companies are private i.e. their shares are not available for the public to invest in and these employ less than 50 people. Some companies in this 'unquoted' group are wholly-owned subsidiaries of listed corporations.

Associations of individuals pursuing a common charitable or not for-profit purpose are found outside of the private sector - but many of these are also incorporated.

Corporate variety

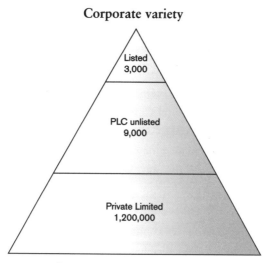

figure 3.1 Corporate Variety

The burgeoning Third Sector

There are around 600,000 associations within the charitable and not for-profit sector of which around 200,000 of these are registered charities. Registration of a charitable body with the Charities Commission in England and Wales requires applicants to provide, in addition to their constitutional documents, information about their actual or proposed activities, plans for funding and trading, and the names of their trustees.

Many of these organizations enjoy healthy standards of governance precisely because their boards share a common and binding social, communitarian or charitable purpose so that they are highly motivated and believe passionately in what they are doing. It is such unity of purpose in the 'Third' and voluntary sectors that has much to offer as an example to struggling companies in the private sector which can sometimes lack strongly held convictions about what they need to achieve. As with the private sector, there is a great concentration of resources and revenues in the top 1% of charities who are more professional and entrepreneurial in their organization and fund raising and these received over 33% of the total funds received by all registered charities. There are, in addition, an enormous variety of organisations which do not have charitable status, but operate primarily for a social rather than an economic purpose. The vast majority of these also choose not to distribute profits to their investors. They include:

- Small, community-based groups
- Organisations working for their members
- Some employee-owned businesses

It has been estimated (**Strategy Unit, Cabinet Office**) that there are approximately 180,000 - 360,000 community level organisations in the UK, for example, hobby clubs, community shops and youth groups, with typically low levels of income and assets, but with high levels of participation and membership. Such organisations can be extremely important in building trust and cohesion in communities, and in developing the skills of those involved in running them. It is estimated that 750,000 individuals serve as trustees within the Third Sector - many without financial reward or compensation!

The diagram shown below (**Strategy Unit, Cabinet Office**) helps to map out the 'Third Sector' and how it overlaps and intertwines with the public, private and charity sectors.

The Third Sector

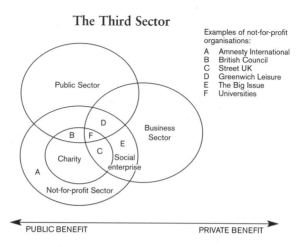

Examples of not-for-profit organisations:

A Amnesty International
B British Council
C Street UK
D Greenwich Leisure
E The Big Issue
F Universities

figure 3.2 *Third Sector Variety Adapted from a model developed by University College London and the New Economics Foundation.*

The beginning of governance obligations

For all these unincorporated groups - whether a charity, sole trader, partnership or community group - there may come a time when they face special difficulties which is when they may wish to expand their activities, raise finance, establish lines of credit, enter into contracts or lease property. A group of individuals who come together to incorporate do so for three practical reasons:

To reduce risk

To enable them to borrow money

To ensure continuity

Anyone can form a private limited liability company but they must meet the following conditions:

• They must not be disqualified from doing so because of previous business malpractice or business failure under the Directors Disqualification Act or the Insolvency Act

• They must not be an undischarged bankrupt

The law is discerning about the probity of the backgrounds of individuals. A private limited company must have a minimum of one shareholder, one director and a company secretary. Once the Memorandum and Articles, the statement of the capital of the company and the registered office, names of directors and shareholders are lodged with the Registrar of Companies then the formation of the company is complete and a certificate of the company's incorporation is issued by Companies House.

The company must then maintain a registered office upon which legal documents can be served. For many of the 1.2 million incorporated companies this is as far as it goes. For others it is the beginning of an exciting journey of growth and development. The prestige and credibility of trading as a company are important reasons for establishing a company but the 'Ltd' part of the company's corporate title also serves as a warning to potential unsecured creditors that the company may not have sufficient funds to repay its debts to them.

The company limited by guarantee

Charitable status by itself does not suggest or require incorporation, neither is it a legal form, but the words themselves represent a helpful title which engenders trust with the public. However, to obtain the protections outlined above, charities and other Third Sector organisations should also consider incorporation for the same reasons as private for-profit companies: It offers a measure of protection from creditors and reassurance to donors. One common form of this type of limited status is the company limited by guarantee which is defined in the Companies Act as: "A company having the liability of its members limited by the Memorandum to such amount as the members may respectively thereby undertake to contribute to the assets of the company in the event of its being wound up." Thus the CLG is characterized as follows -

•   The company carries no share capital

•   The company members guarantee to make a contribution to debts if the company ceases trading

•   The contribution is nominal - usually £1

•   The board is accountable to the founding members

Although many charities choose to incorporate themselves as Companies Limited by Guarantee this legal form was not designed for charities and does not differentiate sufficiently clearly the requirements of company law and charity law. Anyone who is a member of the board of a charitable company is both a company director and a charity trustee.

It is unclear precisely the way in which the duties imposed on directors by company law overlap with the duties imposed on trustees by charity law and, where there is a conflict, which takes precedence. There are specific proposals being made at present by the Government to introduce a new variety of company for charities which would be designed to overcome these inconsistencies - to be called the 'Charitable Incorporated Organisation'.

Case Study: Tynemouth Enterprise Trust

Tynemouth Enterprise Trust was incorporated in 1988 as a company limited by guarantee; it formed part of the burgeoning enterprise trust movement across the UK. In a blaze of publicity the founding members of the Trust outlined their commitment to encourage new business start-ups and a sense of entrepreneurship in what was an area of industrial decline and high unemployment. The founding members included two major manufacturers who were 'downsizing' and wanted to provide work opportunities for their former employees. The local council were also members and provided valuable working capital and premises at a favourable rent. There was a genuine sense of excitement and corporate social responsibility as the new company opened its doors for trading and the newly constituted board got to grips with the task in hand. The founding members provided senior members of staff to be nominated to the board. Grants were won from the various government agencies to fund staffing and overheads and a Business Loan Fund was established to help provide start-up finance. After 15 years much had been achieved - the area had been transformed from a 'brown-field' area to an attractive business location for business start-ups. The problem was that the whole area of business services and advice to the start-up market had become increasingly competitive and cost sensitive. Government funding was subject to competitive tender and the board had lost much of the original enthusiasm and 'spark' as the founders had moved on. In addition the P&L was showing losses after years of generating surpluses and the situation looked unlikely to improve. The balance sheet contained substantial reserves but the board was becoming increasingly concerned about the role and viability of the company.

Issues

*   In the light of the concept of 'immortality' what advice would you give the board?

*   To whom is the board accountable - the local community or its members?

- Would it be right for the board to wind up the company and distribute the reserves to the members?

Other innovations in corporate variety

Once companies are formed they are described as having a 'veil of incorporation' drawn around them. They become a legal entity in their own right unlike a partnership which has no separate legal existence and is merely an association of persons carrying on business together with, usually, unlimited liability. There are also a number of more exotic forms of corporate body which are used for special purposes; owners and founders of corporate bodies need to be aware of these innovations so that they can match their own special business or charitable objectives to the most suitable corporate form which will take into account individual liability, registration, reporting and regulatory requirements as well as taxation implications.

Dormant and audit-exempt companies.

When a company has been voluntarily wound up the owners may select to keep the company dormant in terms of meeting future warranties. A company is dormant during a period in which no significant accounting transaction occurs.

Unlimited companies

This is a rare but legitimate form of company. They should not be confused with an unincorporated business. Unlimited companies are separate legal persons. Because creditors have recourse to the owners to meet any unpaid debts then company does not have to publish any accounts. The Brenninkmeyer family from Holland preferred to keep the financial records of C&A private and operate as a private unlimited company.

Limited liability partnerships

The growth of traditional partnerships has been hampered by their unlimited liability status as Arthur Anderson found out to their cost in the wake of the Enron collapse. A new form of company established by law in 2000 - the Limited Liability Partnership has the organisational flexibility and tax status of a partnership, but the partners have limited liability subject to safeguards for those with whom they deal. The LLP format has been used successfully in the Third Sector.

Incorporated by Charter

Some corporate bodies are incorporated by charter. The Institute of Directors and various professional organisations are incorporated in this way.

Incorporated by Statute

Harbour boards and trusts are incorporated under Statute Law, as are organizations such as the Office of Fair Trade.

Subsidiary companies

It is estimated that two-thirds of the registered companies within the UK are controlled by a holding company. Even so, they remain as independent legal entities to which the subsidiary directors owe duties.

Societas Europae

In addition to national private and public companies, from the beginning of 2004 the European Company - 'Societas Europeae' (SE) - will be established. An SE can operate on a European-wide basis and be governed by Community law directly applicable in all Member States. The advantages are that companies established in more than one Member State will be able to merge and operate throughout the EU on the basis of a single set of rules and a unified management and reporting system.

Community Interest Company

The aims of social enteprises are social, rather than to make profits for owners. Their activities are partly charitable and partly commercial; they are ultimately accountable to their users, members or staff, rather than to shareholders. To serve this form of organization it is proposed the establishment of a new corporate variety - the Community Interest Company (CIC). These would be enterprises which use their profits for public benefit. In order to be established as a CIC, its activities would have to be considered by a reasonable person to be of benefit to the community. It would have to show that its products or services would be made available to a wide constituency rather than to an unduly restricted group of beneficiaries. Community Interest Companies would not be able to have charitable status but would be intended as a vehicle for non-charitable social enterprise.

Questions for corporate governors

• Do you appreciate that the company may have limited liability but a director's liability may be unlimited?

• What steps do you need to take as a governor to reduce this risk?

- How does the inherent characteristic of company immortality impact upon the way you govern?

- Who do you envisage will be the company members and owners in 5 years, 10 years and 50 years?

- What can you learn from the Third sector about good governance and what are the implications for your company?

- Should you become involved as a trustee with the Third Sector as part of your development and learning and responsibility to the wider community?

Conclusion

The joint stock company revolutionised the way business is done. The idea that ownership and management could be separated was unthinkable before the Act. It is fundamental to understanding the role and status of a company to appreciate that a registered company is a legal entity in its own right. The model is so robust that organisations within the burgeoning Third Sector adopt the protection that the 'veil of incorporation' provides. Although the company's essential purpose remains absolutely clear - allowing a company of people to come together, to incorporate, for business or commercial reasons - its role and form is continually under scrutiny and potential reform.

It is still a very simple process to establish a company and remains a popular undertaking. The principle that companies should be set up to be immortal has profound implications for the way companies are directed and for the stewardship of these legal entities to which directors owe their duty. For those who do not wish to take on these burdens there is always the option of becoming a sole trader who is unincorporated and trades without the limited liability of an incorporated body but enjoys the advantages of privacy and a more unregulated business environment. There are a variety of corporate formats and their design continues to be modified with the advent of the Limited Liability Partnership, Community Interest Company and the Societas Europae.

CHAPTER FOUR - PUBLIC TRUST IN THE BOARD

"If you take the man as he is you make him worse; if you take the man as he ought to be you make him better" (Goethe)

- The vast majority of honest directors are in danger of becoming unfairly associated with the very few who are not
- Whenever there is a vacuum in public trust it is filled by regulation
- Trust is often a function of understanding and toleration

There is a huge debate going on about trust. This is not only the result of public concerns about, for example, the reliability of the Press or the government's PR operation, but also about the extent to which we are able to trust our institutions in both the public and private sectors. Examples of corporate scandal and greed - whilst appearing to be mainly amongst larger corporations - has tainted the way we think about all companies, large and small, public and private and about the way we think about the directors who are in charge of them. We appear not to trust directors and, as Goethe pointed out, the more we take this untrusting stance the worse directors appear to behave and the more we will end up regulating them and removing from them their natural desire to be good stewards.

One survey after another has highlighted the ways that individuals are highly suspicious of those in whom they should, or have, placed their trust; those who society has always assumed can be trusted and those in whom we have faith: Faith that they will act always professionally and to the highest standards of personal and professional integrity.

Amongst these results are:

- 30% of respondents thought that business leaders generally tell the truth compared to doctors (92%), scientists (69%) and the ordinary man/woman in the street (55%)
- 9% of respondents were 'very satisfied' with the way that Accountants do their jobs compared to nurses (55%) and teachers (34%)
- In 1970 the public agreed by a majority of 2 to 1 that 'the profits of companies help to make things better'. In 1999, the public by 2 to 1 disagreed.
- In 1970, 75% agreed that 'a company with a good reputation would not sell poor products. In 1999, only 58% think this is so.
- 75% of respondents thought that directors of large companies are paid too much.

- 80% of respondents did not agree with the statement 'directors of larger companies can be trusted' and a similar number (78%) felt that 'directors of larger companies are paid too much for the job they do'. (MORI 1999-2004)

These examples suggest that contemporary culture simply does not trust and that directors are one of the groups with a limited stock of trust with the public. People are in danger of losing their trusting gene! The result is an increasing burden of regulation; the risk of individuals becoming unwilling to take up their directorial roles and even the development of a governance culture which believes that directors are not in the business of good governance at all: That by removing their obligation for making sound decisions and creating 'right relationship' with others as a voluntary activity, they can leave their duty of faithfulness to others, which is the very foundation of their role!

This loss of public trust erodes one of the principal aims of the limited company which is to ensure that directors owe a duty of faithfulness, or 'fiduciary duty' to the company they serve.

The investor-shareholder-owners and other stakeholders have all placed their trust in the directors they have appointed and their trust assumes that directors will clearly understand this and will act with faithfully towards it:

- **That the company is the person to whom faithfulness is owed and with whom directors should develop a 'right relationship' of trust**

- **That it is in the language used to define this relationship that gives it meaning and that this meaning changes continually as the relationship grows and the company develops**

- **That by acting in good faith - by discharging the trust placed upon them by others - directors can build more trust which is a key attribute of successful companies**

- **That an individual director makes his or her journey towards becoming a trusted and faithful governor and that this takes much time and effort - there are no easy answers or ready made solutions**

The F-word

As we have seen, the first duty of a director or trustee of a corporation is the duty of faithfulness or the 'fiduciary' duty that he or she owes to the company or organisation. Within the Companies Act there is an expectation that the director will act in good faith. Corporate governance is partly about ensuring that this 'good faith' is both at the heart of the collective deliberations of the board and that the individual directors' understanding of this duty is created and maintained.

This duty of faithfulness cannot be conjured out of the air; it needs to be learned and earned. This learning comes not only from a set of guiding principles that have been developed over many centuries, from many different cultural influences and in many different circumstances but also as a part of our belonging in today's world and in the language that is used which gives ourselves and our actions meaning.

The next two chapters develop the theme of putting the F-Word back into governance and examining the principles, language and meaning of the words faith, faithfulness, duty and trust as one way to understand how directors can act faithfully in governance. The use of language and the spoken delivery of words are the basic skills and tools of boardroom activity and directors need to ensure that these are carefully defined and crafted and introduced with care and precision.

Meaning what is said

When we say that this or that individual can be 'trusted'; he or she did not act 'in good faith'; that person is an 'honest' individual or they are 'speaking the truth', we are giving meaning to certain types of behaviour through language and by doing so we are also helping to define them. When was the last time the Board of which you are a member had a discussion about the meaning of such words as:

- **Trust**
- **Acting in good faith or acting in bad faith**
- **Honesty**
- **Truthfulness,**
- **Integrity**
- **Transparency**

and what behaviour do you associate with them? Have any of the Boards to which you belong ever tested the levels of mutual recognition, understanding and meaning that these words have for you and for the colleagues with whom you work?

Experience suggests that when everything is going well, clarity about such words is not a priority - although lack of it can frustrate attempts to achieve an even higher performance without being aware of the reasons for mediocrity.

When things are going badly however - or when extra effort is required for either greater success or mere survival, and if attention has not been given to developing the attributes of trustfulness, or if they are unclear, then such lack of clarity and common understanding of the importance of shared governance values can destroy companies and organisations.

The person in law - which is the company - has to be more than the sum of its parts who are its shareholders, just as the Board as a whole has to be more than the sum of its members, who are the individuals who act as its directors, or it will have no purpose or future. Individual directors, acting out of faithfulness on behalf of their company, have, therefore, a unique part to play to ensure the success of the enterprise in which they hold responsibilities.

Opportunity for insight

On certain occasions this collective responsibility for success may become problematic, for example, when one or a number of directors may be thinking about organising a management buy out and place their own future interests above those of the company; when one or more director has an interest in a property which is let to the company and their duty to the company becomes of less importance than their interest in personal gain or when a charity is managed by a charismatic founder-director-trustee and his or her own vision takes over or dominates any potential for corporate aspirations so that the charity becomes that individual's personal fiefdom.

Equally, using the 'diffused' or 'stakeholder' model of corporate governance, there may be a breakdown of trust between directors and their stakeholders. The Forelands Ports Case Study below is an example of what happens when the trust and confidence needed to lead a company is absent and the action raised by the policyholders of Equitable Life is another. In the public sector the breakdown in trust between, for example, the doctors and managers at the Bristol Royal Infirmary and the parents of the children whose bodies had been used without their permission for research led to deep distress for the families involved and to widespread public outrage.

Case Study: Forelands Ports Co. Ltd.

Forelands Ports, own and operate port facilities including a ferry terminal in the Firth of Forth. It was set up as a non-profit distributing trust in 1841 and its directors act as its trustees who are drawn from amongst local stakeholders. Governance issues began to emerge two years ago when a major new port development project went over budget. A number of the trustee-directors felt that external help was needed to review the Board's existing governance practice and to consider ways in which it could be improved. Amongst the issues that had been identified as needing attention were: The role of the Board (confidence, respect and trust); the role of the director (qualities needed, conflicts and confidentiality) and the decision making process (clarity of purpose, communications and direction). A Whole-Board development process was facilitated but half way through the day it had not yet been possible to tackle some of the deeper issues, which were the underlying causes of the apparent dysfunction of the Board.

A questionnaire was circulated which invited each of the directors to rate the way they felt about a number of issues on a scale of 0-5, which included their assessment of Board values such as tradition v flexibility, collaboration v competition, conflict v co-operation, control v inclusivity, relationships v special interests and communication v secrecy. The results were plotted onto a graph and it was clear to all present that the Board had major issues that it would need to resolve in order to improve its performance. A way had to be found for strongly held feelings about trust-mistrust and involvement-exclusion to be expressed as a part of a learning process. The directors were asked to describe the meaning they ascribed to the word trust by completing the sentence 'I understand trust as.....' or 'For me trust is.......' The responses included:

- *Giving my best*
- *Honesty*
- *My bond*
- *Reliable*
- *Openness*
- *Integrity*
- *Transparency*
- *Respect.*

The same process was done for the word 'involvement' and the responses were:

- *'Having a say"*
- *Commitment*
- *Sharing decisions*
- *Participation*
- *Listening*
- *Debating*

This process helped the directors to see not only how things really stood between them (bad) but also how they would like things to be in the future (good) and opened up the prospect of a new reality of working better as a team.

Discussion points

- I understand trust as ....?
- Other board members understand trust as................................?
- I understand involvement as ....?
- Other board members understand involvement as......................?

When truthfulness and integrity are not present between and amongst directors, how is an individual director or trustee to respond? Does he or she become known as a member of 'The awkward squad' or resign in despair? Board members should encourage open dissent and awkwardness - this is a sign of a healthy board. Debates over failures in truthfulness and integrity are at the heart of governance and should be encouraged. If board members are constantly agreeing on matters of principle then the balance of the board is wrong; if two board members are in constant agreement then perhaps one should go!

Standards of public trust

Over the years there have been many attempts to define how individuals acting on behalf of others - that is, discharging their duty of trust - should behave. One of the best known is Lord Nolan's seven principles of public life which he set out whilst chairing the Committee on Standards in Public Life (**Nolan**) which was set up as a result of abuses by MPs of their parliamentary privileges. These principles include:

- *Selflessness:* Holders of public office should take decisions solely in terms of the public interest. They should not do so in order to gain financial or other material benefits for themselves, their family or their friends.

- *Integrity:* Holders of public office should not place themselves under any financial or other obligation to outside individuals or organisations that might influence them in the performance of their official duties.

- *Objectivity:* In carrying out public business, including making policy appointments, awarding contracts, or recommending individuals for rewards and benefits, holders of public office should make choices on merit.

- *Accountability:* Holders of public office are accountable for their decisions and actions to the public and must submit themselves to whatever scrutiny is appropriate to their office.

- *Openness:* Holders of public office should be as open as possible about all the decisions and actions that they take. They should give reasons for their decisions and restrict information only when the wider public interest clearly demands.

- *Honesty:* Holders of public office have a duty to declare private interests relating to their public duties and to take steps to resolve any conflicts arising in a way that protects the public interests.

- *Leadership:* Holders of public office should promote and support these principles by leadership and example.

In a survey carried out for the Audit Commission by MORI, individuals were asked to identify 3 qualities which they felt were important in (public) leaders:

Honest:	38%
Trustworthy:	37%
Good communicator:	26%
Competent:	24%
Experienced:	19%
Accessible:	18%
Integrity:	18%
High moral standards:	16%
Professional:	16%
Efficient:	15%

Trust and boardroom pay

These are high standards to meet and may represent a challenge for directors in the private sector. One issue that has created public mistrust has been that of boardroom pay in large companies. The level of reward for directors can be real test of faithful behaviour. In a market economy, property rights rest with the owners and they should be the arbiters of the level of reward. A share in a company is a share in property rights. Power may be delegated to the board - or to one of its committees to decide issues of director's pay but this should be ratified by the owners as a part of a transparent process - usually at the AGM. In the past, boards and their committees have failed to consult with their owners on this vital aspect of governance but recently owners have been insisting upon their rights by overturning the board's decisions on executive pay. For example, in March 2004 owner pressure - applied by the Association of British Insurers, representing institutional investors - forced Mitchells & Butlers, Compass and First Choice into U-turns on plans to pay bonuses to directors who had not met performance payment requirements.

Trust and performance

One of the key discussions at the board will be about trust because trust is an essential ingredient for sustainable success and will need to be created and nurtured. Trust is a part of the company's intangible assets and another form of capital. Trust encourages openness and 'right relationship'. Trust shows care and concern and provides support and recognition. Trust is a key ingredient for successful leadership. If there is low trust there will evidence of risk avoidance at the board and a reluctance to consider new ideas. Trust helps co-operation and confidence to develop and from trust loyalty and faithfulness can be created.

Public trust is not only therefore about the standards of behaviour expected of individuals in positions of power, authority and responsibility but also about the way that these standards can be created and maintained. The trust that individuals place in institutions takes time to mature through the reputation that is accreted over time but unless trust is maintained continually it can be destroyed quickly and suddenly. Good governance is about having directors who are constantly alert to changing influences and perceptions of the company or organisation which may affect the level of trust within it so that risk can be minimised and reputation enhanced.

Questions for corporate governors

How does your board perform?

	YES	NO
We work on building trust		
We have a model of 'right relationships'		
We are not bound by 'no poaching' agreements		
We can say what we mean, and mean what we say		
We effectively induct and include new directors		
We accept that independent directors need to meet without the executive directors		
We embrace transparency rather than secrecy		
We take stock of trust as a company asset		

Table 4.1 How does your board perform?

Conclusion

The public's trust in all institutions is in decline. Companies are not immune from this trend and directors are targeted as untrustworthy. This means that whatever directors may plan and do, there will be suspicion about their motives. Issues of boardroom pay not only generate envy but an overriding suspicion that directors are 'feathering' their own nests rather than furthering the interests of the company that they are appointed to serve. This can lead to dissatisfaction not only within the company and by its employees but also amongst its stakeholders and particularly its customers.

Directors need to appreciate that in their faithfulness to the company they are fulfilling a vital role that not only sustains the long term viability of their company but also helps to sustain the fabric of society.

CHAPTER FIVE - PRIVATE FAITH AT THE BOARD

• All directors require an appreciation of the meaning of their fiduciary duty

• Acting in 'good faith' is not a 'bolt-on' option - it is the essential driver of director performance

• Meanings of 'faith' and 'faithfulness' are continually changing, often beyond our comprehension

• If we are unable to be trustful, we will find it more difficult to be loyal; if we are unable to be loyal, we will find it more difficult to be faithful

• 'Faith in' has to be built and nurtured within the boardroom; it does not just happen!

Public trust cannot be separated from private faith. Long before we make judgements about which institutions are trustworthy and which cannot be trusted, we have learned the ways of trustfulness and of faithfulness and will be able to appreciate their value in our lives and the distinction we have to make between trust and mistrust. Such appreciation will help us to freely associate with others, to undertake activities in right relationship with them and to develop those attributes that are needed to form the basis for the bonds for which the act of incorporation into a company is intended. Loyalty and faithfulness are a consequence of trust. If we cannot trust, we will find it difficult to be loyal and if we cannot be loyal, we will find it impossible to be faithful and fulfill the 'fiduciary' role, the role of faithfulness, to which directors are appointed.

• From where does the development of 'faith in.........' come from?

• How can faithfulness be created and maintained in individual lives?

• How can 'faith in'.... and faithfulness become the norm in the boardroom?

Cultural roots

The story of faithfulness - and the way we understand it - has a long history which involves individual experience, the story of history and cultural settings.

The motto of the City of Worcester is 'Fides' or 'faithful' to commemorate the faithfulness of its people to the Royalist cause through six years of civil war between 1648-1654. The duty owed to a company by its directors demands a similar faithfulness and the words 'faith', 'trust' and 'fiduciary' have the same Latin root: 'Fides', meaning 'faithful'. 350 years ago, the meaning of 'faithful' would have been commonly understood but in contemporary culture it can have more than one meaning or has become discredited through its association with religious faith or fanaticism. An important aspect for the development of good governance is therefore about our understanding of these words and the meanings that are attributed to them in contemporary culture.

Faith and upbringing

This matters not only because it will influence the way that individuals think about corporate governance but also in the way that a collective understanding of the meaning of the key words associated with faith and trust will be created and maintained. This in turn will influence the way that individuals behave and how standards will develop. One result of negative experiences in life is that it can limit the meaning of the word 'faithful' for individuals who have experienced, for example, family disruption, and could produce a society of crabbed individuals who trust neither themselves nor others. Alternatively, individuals who have had experiences from which they have learned to trust and to have faith in themselves and others, for example, an excellent class room teacher, will be more likely to develop skills of co-operation and to help to contribute as citizens to a society whose features include the willingness to share resources, an openness to the possibility of change and of taking responsibility for what happens in the world. This is not unlike the attributes of an ideal chairman of a company as he or she seeks to get the best from the other members of the board!

Contemporary faith

In contemporary culture, there are particular pressures which suggest that 'faith in........' and 'trust in........' are being diminished, for example, in the confusion surrounding national education curriculum examination results, so that individuals feel that they are surrounded by the untrustworthy and by those in whom they cannot have faith-in or place their trust-in. For example, in his book 'Ministries of Deception', Tim Slessor (**Slessor, T.**) describes how successive governments, and their civil servants, will always try to prevent the truth being known if it would cause either their Minister or their departments embarrassment, or worse. Slessor claims that the implications for returning military personnel of Gulf War syndrome in

1992 and the refusal of the government to reveal all of the facts or take any responsibility for the RAF Chinook helicopter disaster in 1994, are two examples of the way that public confidence in individuals and institutions which were formerly held as trustworthy has been eroded. Whilst the conclusions of Lord Hutton's enquiry into the death of Dr. David Kelly exonerated the Government of any wrongdoing, they have not restored confidence in authority and the episode is only the latest example of a trend towards mistrustfulness.

Slessor writes: 'Could the answer be that secrecy is very close to power and that information denied to others is, in itself, a boost to a feeling of authority'. This statement introduces three further aspects of meaning closely related to trust and faithfulness: The power and authority that is often the companion to those exercising governance and the leadership associated with it each of which will be discussed in Chapters 7 and 8.

Openness.......

In his contribution to the book 'Open Government - What do we need to know?', Gerard Hughes introduces the idea of the common good as being one way to indicate the presence of trust and to test this by asking the question: 'To what extent can we trust that the common good is being pursued on any specific occasion?'(**Hughes, G.**) The idea of the common good is one drawn from Athenian society and combines the interests of the individual citizen with that of the city state or commonwealth. The question of what is the common good is answered 'first by the individual and then by society'. (**Hollenbach, D.**) Hughes goes on to remark that: 'Those who wield power will inevitably find it in their interest to cover up their mistakes since such revelations will weaken the security of their hold over power in the longer term'. One purpose in having rules of governance is therefore to ensure that both public and private interests are considered so that they can witness to justice being done and the common good being maintained by the company.

.... v Secrecy

Secrecy in government is not the only way in which trust and faith in other people and institutions can be eroded, which is another feature of contemporary culture.

In her 2002 Reith lectures, Onora O'Neill provided evidence that, whilst we may not be in a crisis of trust, there is a growing culture of suspicion about those who govern.

She offered three reasons for this:

- New concepts of accountability, particularly in the public sector, which encourage spurious reporting

- The age of transparency through IT which pretends wider participation whilst often deceives by conveying only that information which is convenient

- A culture in the public and political arena which prides itself on its own standards but is often suspicious of everyone else's. (**O'Neill, O.**)

Developing faith

These trends all place pressure upon the meaning of trust; the attributes associated with its meaning and therefore the nature of the faith which individuals will bestow, either willingly as individuals or unwillingly as members of society, upon others who exercise power and authority, ultimately, on their behalf. This increasingly diffused understanding of such key words as 'trust' and 'faith' and the meanings given to them by contemporary culture can also affect the faith that each individual places upon him or herself. Trust or faith in governance can therefore take at least three forms:

- An individual's understanding of faith and the meaning they give to it which comes from their learned experience of it.

- The way an individual's understanding may or may not be in tune with the meaning of trust and faith used within the corporate body, company and organisation of which the individual is a member.

- The way that faith and faithfulness is interpreted and regulated by society in order to meet the needs of the common good.

In order for good governance to flourish, all three of these aspects need to be represented. The recognition that faith and trust are important to ensure that individual, corporate and common good aims are met, means that there is a need to understand how such faith and trust can be created, fostered and maintained.

Stages of faith

One way to approach how 'trust in....' and 'faith in.......' can be understood is to look at some theories about how this quality can occur. In his book 'Stages of Faith' James Fowler, a notable social psychologist in the USA, writes about the way that faith develops and, using the theories of other members of his discipline, for example, Piaget, Kohlberg and Erikson, all of whom developed their own models of the stages of human development from infancy to maturity, he re-interprets their work in trust and faith language. (**Fowler, J.**)

For example, in his analysis of the adolescence stage of an individual he writes: 'Where social conditions and favourable personal relationships support young persons in building a firm enough sense of identity to feel ready to commit themselves in friendship - to future work roles or in loyalty to religious or other ideological visions and communities - we may expect in them the virtue we call fidelity'. It seems then that human beings have a 'generic vocation - a universal calling' for the creation of relationships of trust and loyalty which gives deep meaning and importance to up-bringing and early experiences of trust and faithfulness.

This suggests that as individuals grow and mature they accrete positive or negative interpretations through their experience of the attributes they associate with faith, which can either build up their 'trust-in......' and 'faith in........' or diminish it. Depending upon the outcome, they will have a capacity to trust others or not; have faith in others or not, find it easy to give their loyalty or not. These experiences can have profound consequences for the kind of governors they will become with these positive or negative feelings underpinning their thoughts and actions.

If their experiences have all been negative, such individuals can end up trusting neither themselves nor other people and their impact upon the board and its work can be likewise. A board without 'trust in......' and 'faith in......' will be a board that by definition does not work!

Students of human nature

Understanding the way that human beings develop can help all those who practice governance to appreciate not only the nature of the duty of faithfulness laid upon them, but, also something of the forces that drive individuals. In this way they can help others to make more informed and balanced decisions about the issues of governance that constantly arise.

In addition, whilst it may still be possible to understand faith and faithfulness in a traditional way, in an increasingly secular culture - and one in which there is no agreed language to define the key words which are of such vital importance to the practice of governance - there is a need to search for new language and to create new meanings so that the words that lie at the heart of the governance task find can new expression and relevance.

Historically 'faith in....' has had both a secular and sacred meaning. In the secular, 'faith in....' has been about the way that human beings develop their 'trust-in......' faculty; their 'faith in....' both themselves and others; how this can be nurtured and how it can be damaged. In the sacred, individuals affirmed the part of a creative spirit. For people of religious faith, the tradition from which the 'fiduciary' duty comes - faith in governance - represents both secular and sacred, spirit and humanity, the individual and the corporate, working together.

Progressing in faith

Faith and trust - as a 'generic feature of human lives and as a universal quality of meaning making - pre-potentiates us for faith'. Such faith-making, with its patterns of trust and loyalty, has three attributes: It promotes standards; it creates the images and realities of power and it develops a core story which helps to develop a mature faith. Each individual's faith 'story' comes from their personal history of living through the good times and the bad and, over time - and from this rich variety of experience - these qualities of formation make individuals who they are. These qualities will include humility in the face of adversity and personal modesty in the face of success. It is in these interchanges that our 'faith in.....' becomes deeper and our governance skills develop.

Questions for corporate governors

Auditing board trust

	Agree strongly disagree strongly			
	1	2	3	4
I can contribute freely in boardroom discussions				
I go into board meetings fully prepared				
I come out of board meetings with a clear view on what has been decided				
I trust my colleagues to act in the best interests of the company				
I work on building trustful relationships				
I am faithful to my role as a director				
I respect my colleagues				
I respect myself				
I am not afraid to ask if I do not understand anything				

Table 5.1 Auditing board trust

Conclusion

This process can be thought of as a journey into faithfulness as individuals experience a deeper faith both in ourselves and towards others. This suggests that faith is dynamic and open to change; that learning good governance is a vital part of the process and individuals have within them the ability and opportunity to learn new and un-learn old meanings of what faithfulness means. Education and learning then become key roles in governance because governance is dynamic and changes in the language of governance means changing governance itself. The role of education in governance, the way that existing levels of trust and confidence can be assessed and the key role that the chair of the board has to develop trust will be discussed in Chapter 9.

CHAPTER SIX - THE DIRECTOR AS THE 'GOOD STEWARD'

- Stewardship means to hold the company's assets in trust for its owners - this is the guiding principle for corporate governors

- Part of the collective 'stewardship' role of the board is to lead the company into the future, to set guiding principles, assure executive performance and to embrace accountability for these actions

- Accountability is tough - it means directors having to deliver on their promises - everything else is wishful thinking

- The director is a professional - and should always seek to strive for excellence in stewardship

- Being a good steward is not just about conformance to governance standards it is also about performing creatively to the highest possible standards as a director

- Can corporate social responsibility be compatible with good stewardship?

The story of the good steward who used his talents according to his ability can provide a helpful image for aspiring corporate governors. In fact there were two 'good stewards'- one who received five talents and the other two. It is the faithfulness of the two stewards who take on their responsibilities and do their best for their master that is the purpose of the story. They were not forced to undertake their task - they chose to carry them out to the best of their ability. The lesson that storyteller wanted his listeners to hear was that no matter how well constructed the architecture of corporate governance may be, it requires good 'stewardship' on the part of individual directors who want to breathe life into the work of the board, to take on accountability with a passion and to make governance effective.

All directors should regard themselves as stewards of the talents and gifts they have received and will need to account for them. They should not let them lie idle and even less should they abuse them for the purpose of self-interest or wrong-doing. The two stewards in the Bible story who used their talents well and made a profit for their master are praised and rewarded. When the master returns he says to them: "Well done, good and faithful servants; you have been faithful over a little, I will set you over much; enter into the joy of your master." In the same story, the servant who buried his talent and left it lying idle in the ground is condemned and thrown into the darkness. (**Matthew 25 14-30**)

In this chapter we explore what it means to be a 'good steward' and the demands this places on directors in the way they should think and act.

The director as a fallible human being

One of the key issues at the heart of governance is the relationship between directors and the owners of the company. The study of this relationship has generated two opposing theories. First, what has come to be known as the 'Agency Theory', which presents the relationship between the company's directors and its shareholders as a principal/agency relationship. This infers that the interests and therefore the behaviour of directors - who are the company's agents in its management - will inevitably not always align themselves with the interests of its owners. As a consequence directors cannot always be relied upon to act in ways that will ensure the best returns to shareholders unless appropriate governance and regulatory structures are put in place.

Agency theory therefore suggests that directors are self-serving, individualistic and, in economic terms, will act as utility 'maximisers'. That is, they will maximize returns to themselves. The rules of Governance such as the separation of the CEO and chairman roles and the independence of non-executive directors are therefore designed to provide checks upon the self-serving interests of executive directors. These checks and balances are necessary - so the agency theory goes - to restrain such individualistic motivations and represent a cost upon the owners to ensure 'good' behaviour.

Other costs can also include 'bonding' costs such as bonus and incentive payments linked to the company's share price which also seek to align the interests of the agent - the director - with the interests of the shareholder - the owners. Agency theory therefore stresses individual opportunism, suggests inherent distrustfulness and leads to the need for outside monitoring and control. This results in both the over-governance of these supposedly untrustworthy characters and the use of excessively generous incentives, for example, 'golden hellos' and 'handcuffs' in order to 'buy' their good behaviour.

This approach to ensuring good governance suggests that human beings will behave in inherently selfish ways unless they are constrained and cannot be trusted to act on behalf of others in a spirit of service and duty. This is a Machiavellian idea in its cynicism and disbelief in the higher and more noble aspirations of humankind. Little wonder that those who believe this Agency Theory of governance view corporate governance as a controlling device designed to restrict the opportunism of directors who if left to their own devices, will only serve their own interests! Agency theory expects the worst and plans for it.

Stewardship theory

Stewardship theory, on the other hand, defines situations in which directors are not driven by self interest but rather are stewards whose motives are aligned with the objectives of their principals - who are the shareholders. Stewardship theory is founded in Judeo-Christian history and psychological study rather than the law and economics. Stewardship theory focuses on non-quantifiable, and other less intangible ways to reward stewards instead of tangible rewards such as their level of remuneration. The focus of this theory is that a good steward will have an attitude of service towards his or her owner-shareholders and an interest in the greater good of the company as a whole.

Stewardship theory recognizes a range of non-financial motives for the behaviour of director/stewards. These include: The natural aspiration for achievement and recognition, the intrinsic satisfaction of successful performance and a respect for authority from others and for the work ethic. In other words, stewardship is "the willingness to be accountable for the well being of the larger organization by operating in service, rather than in control, of those around the organization" (**Block, P**)

Some of the characteristics of the Agent-theory director compared to the Stewardship-theory director are listed in Table 6.

Agent v steward

Agent	Steward
Serves self interest	Serves the company
Pays lip-service to accountability	Embraces accountability
Believes pay schemes are pivotal to organizational successes	Believes learning is pivotal to organizational successes
Focuses on hierarchy	Focuses on stakeholders
Believes in secrecy	Committed to openness
Directs by rules and procedures	Directs by principle
Favours control and enforcement	Favours the learning process
Believes in selective communication	Believes in open communication
Serves self	Serves others
Emphasizes concentration of board power	Emphasizes the need for board balance
Opportunistic and pragmatic	Demonstrates moral courage
Rewards compliance and loyalty	Rewards innovation and personal growth

Table 6.1 *Agent v steward*

Discussion points:

- Do you feel that you act as an Agent or as a Steward?
- What are the difficulties in fully embracing the stewardship model of being a director?
- What personal actions can you take to become an even more effective 'good steward'?
- How can you handle colleagues who do not share your ideas of stewardship?

Leading into the future

At the heart of the story of the 'good steward' is what directors do with the responsibility they have been given. The noblest motive in the heart of a faithful servant will be to accomplish as much as possible for the sake of his or her master during his absence. For the board of directors this absence will be the time between each AGM when the owners - the shareholders - will re-assemble to hear the report of their stewards - the directors. Between each of these meetings, directors will decide how they will fulfill their stewardship responsibilities.

If the board can clarify its job responsibilities collectively and in collegiate ways, the task of stewardship will become easier. It is the chairman of the board who should take the lead in this and help to clarify what the board should and should not do. The following activities will always be central to the board's good stewardship-

- Leading the company into the future
- Laying out the guiding principles and policies for the company
- Assuring the performance of the full-time executives
- Embracing accountability at all levels

In the debate about governance it can often be forgotten that the prime role of the director and the board is to lead. John Harvey Jones captured this sentiment when he stated: *"If the board is not taking the company into the future, who is?"* and again, *"The very essence of every board's role is to create tomorrow's company out of todays"*. (**Harvey Jones, J**)

The 'good steward' does not sit tight on the bundle of human, intellectual and capital assets that he or she holds in trust; the 'good steward' seeks to create a future for the company by re-aligning, strengthening, disposing and re-positioning these assets and building upon the forces of change. The primary skill he or she brings to bear is the ability to 'think strategically' and lead the company into a new, visionary future.

All companies have the potential to fail and stewardship is about reducing this risk by creating new and sustainable futures. This requires an ability to think strategically and takes more than the repetitive analysis of today's experience and yesterday's mistakes which can be a feature of so much planning activity.

Perhaps it is this inability to apply the collective mind of the board of directors to 'strategic thinking' which accounts for so much poor performance. At its simplest strategy is about guiding the organization towards its vision of the future or creating tomorrow's company. This is a conceptual and reflective issue, which appears nebulous at first but there are many strategy processes and techniques to help boards of directors in their task, and each individual director needs to achieve the highest standards in 'strategic thinking'.

Attributes of stewardship

There are a number of key attributes suggested by the IOD that the professional director requires (**IOD**):

- *Change-orientation*
  Being alert and responsive to the need for change. Encouraging new initiatives and the implementation of new policies, structures and practices

- *Creativity*
  Generating and recognizing imaginative solutions and innovations

- *Foresight*
  Imagining possible states and characteristics of the company in the future

- *Organisational awareness*
  Being aware of the company's strengths and weaknesses and of the likely impact of the board's decisions upon them

- *Perspective*
  Rising above the immediate problem or situation and seeing the wider issues and implications. Able to relate disparate facts and see all relevant relationships

- *Strategic awareness*
  Being aware of the various factors which determine the company's opportunities and threats

There are many barriers to effective strategic thinking including those shown at Table 6.1. Edward de Bono described thinking as: *"The most valuable human resource"* (**Bono**) and Donah Zohar challenges us to: *"change the thinking behind our thinking - literally, that we learn to rewire our corporate brains."* (**Zohar, D.**) Directors can sometimes appear to be trapped in the world of yesterday and today's problems and are caught up in action and doing rather than renewing themselves and their thinking processes.

Barriers to strategic thinking

Lack of vision

Short 'termism'

Lack of creativity

Lack of process

Too much process

Poor information flow

Unbalanced board

Poor chairmanship

Inadequate analysis

Existing 'mindset'

Inability to challenge assumptions

Failure to get into the 'mind' of the customer

Failure to be driven by customer needs

Failure to monitor and understand technological change

Not enough board time

Rather take action than reflect

Lack of training

No skills set

No evaluation of the barriers

Incorrect environment

Not accessing intermediaries/facilitators

Copying 'template' strategies

History of strategic failure

Table 6.2 Barriers to Strategic Thinking

Questions for discussion

- How much time does your board spend on 'strategic thinking'?
- How can you release more time for strategic thinking?
- How can you develop your skills in strategic thinking?
- What future is your strategy taking you towards?

Ethical principles and policies to guide the company

Although the board is 'accountable' for what goes on throughout the organisation it cannot always be 'responsible' as it will need to delegate its authority downwards and to others who are its executives. The establishment of a set of strategic principles and policies by the board can help to enable the whole organisation to be guided and aligned to a common, company purpose. For example, such principles can enshrine what the company stands for in its dealings with customers, employees, suppliers and the local community who are its stakeholders.

These is much evidence to suggest that companies which enjoy success have developed a set of core principles and policies which remain fixed while their business activities are continually adapting and changing. These principles promote good stewardship for all members of the organisation - whether they are departmental managers, receptionists or assembly line operators because all these employees hold the assets of the company on behalf of the owners in trust. They will be held accountable for how they exercise their responsibilities and use their talents in the same way as the directors.

The key task is to help these staff to understand and positively want to take on their 'stewardship' roles. The issue in adopting and implementing such stewardship principles is that they need to be universally applied. They need to start with the directors and then be cascaded throughout the organisation.

For example: The principle of honesty can sometimes be flouted within organisations with fiddled expenses, taking home office stationary, using e-mail for personal activities and fraudulent sick notes becoming accepted practices. Unfortunately, this culture can often be perceived as originating in the boardroom when directors encourage wage restraint for others but pay themselves over and above the going rate. When this happens there can be a breakdown of integrity, but the problem can be even more serious than this: one feature of contemporary culture is the gradual change from a set of absolute moral standards and good old fashioned virtues into what are known as 'values'.

The devaluation of values

There is a danger that the term 'value' can imply that standards are subjective; can be relative and change according to individual circumstances, cultural settings and organisational needs. When this happens there is a risk that values are no longer based on absolute standards derived from classical virtues but instead end up being based upon feelings, opinions, choices, attitudes, habits, conventions, or anything else which any individual, or cultural group happens to 'value' at any particular time and in any particular circumstance. The catch phrase of Gordon Gekko, the fictional financier in the film 'Wall Street' was: 'Greed is good' - and this attitude can typify this kind of approach.

The problem with the word 'values' is that it can become debased and meaningless because it does not represent the absolute and lasting standards of the good steward. Some commentators go as far as to suggest that "today's organisations are spiritually impoverished, and only when companies find ways to integrate personal belief with organisational values will meaningful change occur." **(J. Mintoff,J.&Denton,E.).** Yes, we are probably tired of those bland and compromising value statements which fail to connect with what the vast majority really hold dear and believe in. The question - how do I engage our people in what we are trying to do with this organisation? - is central to all the deliberations of the board. This is the question that the good steward needs to answer. The Good Steward husbands the human resources at their disposal and turns them into resourceful individuals who are fully engaged in what the organisation stands for and where it is heading.

Remunerating the good steward

One example of the danger in flexible values - and one which has caused much controversy with its suggestions of 'fat cattery' - is the issue of director remuneration. A principle of the free market is that remuneration should be sufficient to attract and retain the directors needed to govern the company successfully. This principle applies across the spectrum. Few football commentators would, for instance, argue against the signing of a new 'striker' on a wage of £60,000 per week if in football idiom they could 'do the business' and score goals. Football supporters are proud to have the best striker such as a Henri or Larsson, but the mention of a £3m pay package for a FTSE 100 CEO raises the hackles of shareholders and the general public alike.

There is good reason for this as recently there has been a massive transfer of company assets from the owners of corporations to its directors through their acquisition of share options. This process provides a director with options to buy shares in his or her company at their current market price; if the price goes up, whether through their own efforts or through the vagaries of the market, they are allowed to buy at this previously agreed option price, re-sell the shares and take the profit. At a time of falling share values and annual profits, this has had the effect of making a minority of directors appear to have double standards: Shareholder pain has been the director's gain.

In addition, when directors have failed to deliver rewards for owners there has too often been no penalty imposed for poor performance and this 'rewarding failure', which can make the pay of directors up to 200 fold the average pay of the employees of the company, has brought all directors into disrepute. One way to deal with such 'flexibilities' has been to strengthen governance standards and recently a number of investment managers in the City of London who are responsible for investing large sums of pensions monies into companies have used their muscle to insist upon greater transparency and disclosure of board remuneration policies. In future it is likely that owners and shareholders will become more active in calling directors to account so that those few directors who find it difficult to maintain the standards expected of them will be encouraged to exercise more restraint and the virtues of good stewardship.

It seems that the remuneration packages of directors have become over-complex and difficult to understand - and they can often appear to be all carrot and no stick. Of course the good steward should be rewarded in parallel with his or her careful husbanding of the assets of others. Owners will be very happy to endorse packages for directors that are fair, transparent and reward success.

The 'good steward' of the story worked towards his master's absolute standards: faithful to his master's interests, responsible for his actions, conscientious, diligent and with a willingness to be held accountable by him. Whilst the 'values' of contemporary culture may be movable, core virtues are unchanging and include:

Virtues	Values
Wisdom	Knowledge
Courage	Self-motivation
Munificence	Social responsibility
Gentleness	Caring
Faith	Value system
Hope	Self-esteem
Charity	Community
Love	Tolerance
Prudence	Risk management
Conscientiousness	Self-development
Magnanimity	Self-awareness

Table 6.3 Virtues v Values

Discussion points

• What enduring virtues do you bring to the board room?

• Which guiding principles do you share with colleagues?

• What is your policy on director remuneration?

• How consistent is this with overall employee remuneration?

Does Corporate Social Responsibility conflict with stewardship?

If stewardship is about holding the company's assets in trust for its owners is there a conflict with also pursuing the aim of looking after other stakeholders which has been exemplified in the set of guidelines which have become associated with the words 'corporate social responsibility'? Business in the Community - one of the leading employer organisations in the UK committed to corporate responsibility - has set out a number of principles which summarises this approach and which include:

• Treating employees fairly, equitably and with respect

• Operating ethically and with integrity

• Respecting basic human rights

• Sustaining the environment for future generations

• Being a responsible neighbour in communities

At face value few organisations would disagree with these principles which involve serving the interests of a variety of stakeholders. But there are some important issues about how a board decides what proportion of its resources should be committed to these 'other' stakeholders and how some of them are more important than others.

There will always need to be a balance struck between the primary aim of the company which is to make profits and the amounts that should be dedicated to CSR activities. Figure 6.3 shows the way one Scottish engineering company, Robert Taylor Holdings Ltd. accounts for the way stakeholders benefited from the disbursement of cash during one financial year. The account shows stakeholder investments made in service providers, employees, lenders, customers, the Community, Government and Shareholders with the final figure of £457,000 being retained in the company for the benefit of its long-term future. This is one way to show how stakeholders can benefit from the activities of a successful and profitable company.

Robert Taylor Holdings Ltd. (consolidated)		
Cash Value Added 1997/98		
CASH GENERATED	£'000	STAKEHOLDER
Sale of products	10,271	Customer
Payment to suppliers & services	5,557	Service Providers
Cash value added	4,714	
CASH UTILISED		
Employee remuneration	2,794	Our Team
State taxes	1,030	Government
Community investment	78	Community
Interest/finance costs	100	Lenders
Dividends	255	Shareholders
CASH DISBURSED	4,257	
CASH RETAINED		
Funding of growth & replacement	457	Company

Table 6.4 Cash Value added Statement for
Robert Taylor Holdings Ltd., with kind permission of Robbie Taylor.

Some commentators have gone so far as to argue that the activity of balancing the interests of various stakeholders allows directors to 'get off the hook' and can become little more than 'embezzling' other people's money. (**Sternberg, E.**)

For Sternberg, directors becoming responsible to stakeholders rather than owners can be incompatible with good governance and that what matters is for directors to pursue their corporate objectives by respecting the principles of 'distributive justice' and 'ordinary decency'. She states that: *"What distributive justice means is simply that those who contribute most to achieving the objective of the organisation deserve most from the organisation.* (**Sternberg,E.**) *"Corporate activities must therefore be conducted with honesty, fairness, the absence of physical violence and coercion, and a presumption in favour of legality. Collectively, these constraints embody what may be called ordinary decency."*

In some respects corporate social responsibility is another 'Third Way' which occupies the space between the free market and state regulation. It is a relatively new idea and directors have to use their judgement in reconciling its activities with the interests of the company's owners. It provides another way for directors to manage risk and reputation as the public becomes increasingly sceptical about the way companies impact on the social fabric and environment. Renato Martino, a cardinal of the Roman Catholic church, at the close of the international Conference of Christian Business Executives, in March 2004 commented: *"Moral values, such as social responsibility, solidarity, justice, a sense of the common good, care of the environment, respect for human rights, the appreciation of human capital are not enemies of economic and business activity, but their most faithful allies, though certainly very demanding."* He also went onto say: *"That the function of the business executive and of an enterprise is to be a reflection of creative action."* (**Martino, R.**)

Questions for corporate governors

YOUR TOMORROW'S COMPANY in Scotland INQUIRY

Please fill in each box with a number 1-5 (1 = least, not doing it or worst, 5 = most, doing it or best)

LEADERSHIP

Do your leaders understand the key relationships upon which success depends? ☐
How clear is your staff about the company's purpose and direction? ☐
How clear is your staff about the company values? ☐
To what extent is your staff encouraged to take a lead themselves? ☐

YOUR STAFF/ASSOCIATES

To what extent are your staff's/associates attitudes measured? ☐
To what extent are values shared and demonstrated by your staff/associates? ☐
To what extent is innovation encouraged in your staff/associates? ☐
To what extent are reward and recognition systems linked to performance and values ☐

YOUR CUSTOMERS

Is the company clear who their key customers are? ☐
To what extent is customer satisfaction measured? ☐
How effective is the process linking measurement to improvement? ☐

YOUR SUPPLIER/BUSINESS PARTNERS (BPs)

To what extent has the company defined success with its suppliers and BPs? ☐
How much trust exists between you and your suppliers and BPs? ☐
To what extent do your suppliers and BPs share your values? ☐

YOUR SHAREHOLDERS

How would you characterise the relationship with shareholders? ☐
Is shareholder loyalty measured and managed? ☐
To what extent are the needs of the other stakeholders explained to shareholders? ☐

YOUR COMMUNITY

How does the community view the company? ☐
Has the company clarified its relationship with its community? ☐
Does the company share resources with the community? ☐
Is there a clear process for how your staff serve the wider community? ☐

WHAT IS YOUR TOTAL OUT OF 100?

HOW FAR ARE YOU ALONG THE TOMORROW'S COMPANY JOURNEY?

Table 6.5 kindly reproduced with the permission of TCIS

Conclusion

The good steward is loyal, shows sound judgement, has high standards and expects to be held to account. The good steward is the model for the good governor and is the alternative to the agent who pursues self-interest and requires to be held in check. The good steward operates to the highest standards of professionalism and seeks to continually raise his or her game.

The collective stewardship of the board requires attention to developing a way forward, establishing principles and policies, supervising the executive and embracing accountability. The inability to think strategically often blocks the work of boards. This skill requires developing and shaping - without it good stewardship can be undermined. The good steward does not hide from accountability; accountability is tough, but the board is expected to deliver on future prosperity - that is why directors are in the position they are. 'Box ticking' on conformance is not stewardship; similarly corporate social responsibility is not stewardship. Stewardship is enterprising and seeks to add value for shareholders.

CHAPTER SEVEN - POWER AND AUTHORITY IN GOVERNANCE

- The way boards govern is a consequence of the way they understand the meaning of power and authority.

- The power and authority of directors is not unrestricted and directors need to explore the boundaries of their roles

- The power and authority of a director over and above others is an almost sacred responsibility for the lives of many people and should always be used constructively and as a feature of 'right relationship' with others.

- Directors need to develop reserves of inner strength which come from practising their power and authority upon which they can draw when they need to create new visions for the future.

- The director who is creative knows that all that is accomplished using their power and authority is achieved through working within constraints: Without constraints to power there is no creating.

This chapter explores the relationship between those who have power and authority with those to whom they are responsible. Finding the right balance between exercising power and authority as 'the' business of the board and the responsibility for the continuing faithfulness owed to others is not easy but when it is achieved provides the basis for 'right relationship', personal and corporate satisfaction and long term success.

There can be no 'pecking order' at the board unless such arrangements have been referred to specifically in the company's M&As, so that each of the directors have equal rights and an equal share of the power and authority given to the board by the shareholders. Should any delegation of power be arranged to, for example, the CEO or Chair, such power comes only from the board collectively and remains with it.

This takes great faith in both self and others and directors need to learn and reflect upon their own experience of power and their understanding of authority in order to develop their skills in power and authority.

As a way to tackle a number of issues related to learning more about power and authority, a variety of meanings are explored below and in particular those that arise from history and culture. Such examples may be half-forgotten but they remain deeply embedded in the way that governance is thought about and have played a significant part in helping to shape our present understanding of power and authority.

Faith - its meaning and the values that are attributed to it which are developed and located within the individual - and which were discussed in Chapters 4 and 5 - is the same faith which is entrusted to those who govern and to directors who hold their power and authority on behalf of others which is the principle function of their role. In corporate governance such individuals often hold their appointment as a director or trustee by election, either by their peers as members of the board or by the votes of investors at the AGM of the company as specified in its Memorandum & Articles.

Whilst the source of this power and authority is therefore usually very clear - from the authentication which comes from their formal appointment as a director - the way that a director places meaning upon his or her personal power-position has an equally important part to play. Alongside their own faith development, their understanding will determine how they will govern and the values they will attach to the role. In other words, each of us can be either a 'good' or a 'bad' governor.

Historic meanings in governance

There are many different models of power and authority available from which to learn both from our own personal experience and from culture and these models will inform the way we will think about how we should discharge our responsibilities as governors. Each director - consciously or unconsciously - will have selected one or more models with which they are familiar or feel comfortable and these will be as a result of many cultural influences. To illustrate this, one example that has influenced society's understanding of power and authority for over four centuries - and given meaning to them - is the story of the consequences of the theory of the Divine Right of Kings in the 17th Century. There are many other examples of the meaning of power and authority and every director will reflect upon their own examples that give meaning for them.

The historic episode in history to which reference has been made represented a struggle between two alternate models of power one which, once gained, could not be held accountable for its actions to others and the alternative that remained always accountable. This theme will be familiar to directors who have struggled to understand and interpret what is going on in the board room on some occasions!

When questions of order arose in 17th Century England, people immediately thought in Biblical terms. In the immediate post-Reformation era, they were told, often from the pulpit, that political authority and private property had been established as a consequence of Man's Fall and, because Man was a sinful creature, order had to be imposed upon him. This meant that all authority should therefore be accepted as divinely ordained. What people heard was what the government - which was for them the King in his Palace - wanted them to hear. However, as the religious and political settlement between King and Parliament began to break down, both sides used the Bible as justification for their positions. For example at the impeachment of the Earl of Stafford in 1641 who was King Charles I's representative in the country, reference was made: 'That the King's little finger should be thicker than the loins of the law', a convenient biblical quotation from the Book of Kings.

As today, both King and Parliament 'spun' their policies continuously and it was from such disputation that James I/VI developed his theory of the Divine Right of Kings in which he claimed that he was answerable to no earthly authority, an idea that the opposing reformers called 'Turk-like' despotism. Nevertheless, James insisted that he should be treated as Adam's heir and the inheritor of Adam's rights over humankind. Likewise, the command to honour father and mother was taken as an injunction to obey the King his appointed officials.

Tyranny & freedom in governance

However, many of his subjects held the view that the King was absolute in some respects but limited in others, such limitation should include the law of the land and the ancient privileges of people and Parliament: In other words, that power had limits. In his speech to the two Houses of Parliament in 1610, King James claimed that: 'Kings are rightly called gods for they exercise a manner of resemblance of divine power on earth'. However, John Lilburne, one of the most radical of the parliamentary reformers, who spent much of his life locked up for sedition, disagreed when he wrote from prison: 'It is impossible for any man, woman or child to be free from the arbitrary and tyrannical wills of men, except those ancient laws and rights be preserved and maintained'. The dispute escalated, pitting the King against his Parliament, and leading ultimately to six years of civil war in which he was finally defeated and the idea of a king's divine right to rule was dead.

Although any permanent constitutional settlement for the country lay far ahead, at the Putney Parish Church debates of 1647, the principle of a universal franchise was first articulated by John Lilburne and his Model Army allies and confirmed by his colleague Col. Rainsborough when he spoke about the rights of the people: 'If we can agree where the liberty and freedom of the people lies, that will do all'.

These essentially Reformation events were a struggle about where power and authority lay. Finally after years of struggle, the paramouncy of the individual's rights in the face of despotism was confirmed and this remains the basis for much of the meaning of power and authority in contemporary culture as well as being the basis for a democratic society. The ways that corporations should be regulated, which were designed over a century later, were founded upon the outcome of these earlier ideas of the origin of power and authority and the rights of the king compared to his subjects.

A variety of meanings in governance

The 20th Century, in particular, has provided a number of alternative and unsavory examples of governance of which the most notorious were communism and fascism. This means that alongside the meaning of power and authority arising from the development of the democratic model, there still lies the alternative, and often seductive models of the authoritarian king, political party or dictator wielding absolute power and authority. These models remain potent sources of current meanings of power which can be used to justify alternative and more autocratic models of governance. Many directors have experienced the behaviour which derives from such models of which perhaps the most notorious was the late Professor Roland Smith of Manchester United and, briefly, British Leyland, who, as chairman, issued a set of instructions to his non-executive directors about the way they should behave at board meetings which included a rule that they could not ask questions at meetings of which the chairman had not received notification in writing in advance!

Because corporate governance is one way that power and authority is exercised and is a part of the story of the origins and uses of power in our history - and has deep roots in it - individuals who exercise authority in governance need to be aware of the different meanings that alternative models of power and authority represent because they will first inevitably fashion their own roles in governance in ways that are based upon their own experience and understanding of them and second that these may clash with their co-members on the board. The practice of good governance should therefore include frank discussion of these different meanings so that directors can be fully aware of the consequences of the governance models they adopt as a board.

Whilst the authoritarian models of centralised power and authority may have lost much of their meaning as our society moves from one in which such over-arching power had value, into a world in which people will '*only acknowledge the authority of those they trust to understand them*', (**Lash, N**) the authoritarian approaches that they represent - and the remaining influence they have upon the way that power and authority can still be thought about - has much appeal for those who still long for the order and discipline which their exercise of this type of power and authority meant.

However, it is generally appreciated that models of power and authority which come from dialogue and communication are more likely to result in the development of the trust and confidence that are needed to lead tomorrow's company than those based upon the more authoritarian model.

Discussion points

• When did your board last discuss its understanding of power and authority; the sources of its power and the limits placed upon it?

• What are your personal models of power and authority which give meaning to your role; are these compatible with the models used by your colleagues on the board; do you feel that their models conflict with your own and does this make them potentially damaging to the company's future?

• Have you ever asked the employees of the company what their understanding of power and authority is and how this may affect their attitudes to their work?

Changing meanings in governance

From the human consequences of the long history of democratisation, and other examples like it, one key conclusion is that contemporary governors cannot remove themselves from the ever changing values of post-modernity; or by clinging on to models of governance which do not speak to its increasingly varied meaning. Directors need to adapt to survive.

What may have been good and acceptable governance in the past will not do today. Language, which has been used in the past to define governance values - and which may have been universally understood then - will not be understood today and behaviour which may have been tolerated in the past - is not acceptable today. Good governance is therefore a continual process of reflection and learning so that governors can appreciate the changes that are occurring in the meaning of the words used in corporate governance today and can respond to them. Anyone wishing to be a good governor needs therefore to be a follower and practitioner of this dynamic and emergent process. Governance is not therefore a skill, which, once learned, will last a lifetime; its practitioners need to refresh their skills continually.

Limitations of authority

Finally, in practice the power of the board is always limited and the collective responsibility of the board for all its actions offers a way to prevent rogue behaviour or the abuse of power by a single or several directors except in exceptional circumstances. Good governance processes and procedures can help to ensure that the board acts always within its powers and in accordance with its M&As. A board would be acting beyond its powers if, for example, its directors borrowed personally from it without this power being available in its M&As and its directors would become individually liable. In practice, such abuses of power can be checked by shareholders at the AGM who can call abuses of power by directors to account.

Questions for corporate governors

Ask each board member to complete the following audit. Consolidate the findings and establish where there is consensus and where there is room for remedial action.

Considerations	5 Very Good	4 Good	3 Ave.	2 Fair	1 Poor
1 board has full and common understanding of their roles and responsibilities					
2 board members understand the organization's mission					
3 structural pattern (board, officers, committees, executive and staff) is clear					
4 board has clear goals and actions resulting from relevant and realistic strategic planning					
5 board attends to policy-related decisions which effectively guide operational activities of staff					
6 board receives regular reports on finances, budgets, performance and other important indicators					
7 Board has clear policy on transparency, conflicts of interest and fairness					
8 board effectively represents the organization to shareholders & stakeholders					
9 board meetings are focused and makes progress					
10 board regularly monitors and evaluates progress toward strategic goals					
11 board regularly evaluates and develops the chief executive and themselves					
12 board has undertaken a risk assessment and monitors progress					
13 each member of the board feels involved and interested in the board's work					
14 The board has the necessary balance of skills to meet the tasks ahead					

Table 7.1 Board Audit

Conclusion

The tradition that power and authority was a privilege that had to be learned before it could be earned, is no longer dominant and power and authority now have many different meanings so that there is no single meaning that directors can use as a guide to their work. What is clear, however, is that what is the norm for society will also apply in corporate life so that the trend is towards increasing levels of participation and democratisation in corporations. As it is appreciated by many companies that their future lies in releasing the creative energies of the brain power of their employees, it follows that power and authority needs to be exercised firmly but fairly always mindful of the sources of that power and the way that authority effects others because it is their responses which will often determine the future success or failure of the company.

CHAPTER EIGHT - LEADERSHIP IN GOVERNANCE

- Directors are called by their vocation to be models of good governance. Leadership is about being a model for those who follow.

- To be successful, leaders need to develop qualities such as reflective practice, commitment, awareness, compassion and vision.

- Leadership is about being in a relationship with those who choose to follow.

- There are many gurus each claiming to have found the secret of good leadership between the pages of their latest book; leaders consciously need to learn and practice their leadership skills using a variety of different sources of inspiration

- One director will be selected to 'lead' the board as its chair and this individual needs the support of the others and the confidence to be able to represent the company to its shareholders and to the wider public

- Leadership is also about developing a set of strongly held beliefs.

The role of the governor is to lead and to be seen to be leading. By its example, the way the board leads will determine the extent that others will follow. One of the key roles for the board is its capacity to lead the changes and adaptations that are needed and without which the corporation will not survive. Change is hard. Change generates uncertainty. Change is painful and there can be losers as well as winners as a consequence of it. One of the sternest tests that the board will face and a mark of its quality will be the way it leads and directs change by discharging its duty of leadership. No individual or board can lead without first developing a clear set of beliefs about leadership that come from a wide variety of sources which include learning, experience and role models. These will include relationships, motivation, rewards and communication with others as well as a self-belief in the virtue of the high performing role of the corporate governor.

Be a model!

There is no aspect of being a governor that is not also about being a leader. By definition, those who have power and authority also lead and have responsibility for leadership. Governance requires the development of leaders, leadership and skills in leading. In his book 'The Fifth Discipline', Peter Senge asserts: *'the core leadership strategy is simple: Be a model!'* (Senge, P.)

There are many different models of leadership which have been used to demonstrate its qualities. In an earlier era such models shared much in common with each other: Alexander the Great, Caesar, Charlemagne, Wellington and Churchill all displayed qualities which included skills in oratory, vision, tenacity and strategy. As well as such secular individuals, the leaders of the great monotheistic religions, Moses, Jesus Christ and the Prophet Muhammad shared recognisable qualities of leadership that would have been understood by all who heard them or read their work.

In the post-modern era however, such secular and religious models have become diffused following not only the terrible consequences of the tyranny of the 20th Century, but also through the increasing individualism of society: My most admired leader is your most hated leader figure. Leadership models now include football club managers and their players, pop stars and TV presenters alongside the Dalai Lama and the late Mother Teresa of Calcutta. There is therefore no longer a single model of leadership to which directors can aspire. Directors need to reach their own conclusions about their preferred model of leadership so that they do not become simply followers of the latest leadership fad and bend under the pressure of events.

Of the many leadership models that have given meaning in history that of the story of God and His dealings with the world and its people still has significant influence in contemporary culture. This is particularly so where these models are based upon principles of faithfulness that originate in the traditions of, for example, Judaism, Christianity and Islam. This is not only because much of our own society's governance still derives from a time when this story was the dominant influence upon individuals' thoughts and actions but also because of the growing influence of so-called 'fundamentalist' cultures which have resulted in the theocratic regimes of, for example, Iran.

In addition, the way that the early Christian Church used the principles of God's laws and the story of its risen leader, Jesus, to organise its corporate life has also influenced governance. The 'corporation' into which the church evolved quickly became the norm of governance practice throughout the known world of the Roman empire - from which it had borrowed the model - and later of the kingdoms of Western Europe and became the basis for all governance as we know it today. This story of the way the church initially practiced a distinctively authenticated leadership model of governance before regressing to a more authoritarian one, is also a salutary lesson for those of us who are directors and whose good intentions can so easily become frustrated or misdirected at times of crisis and confusion! This 'foundational' story of governance - shared by all of the three great mono-theistic religions of Judaism, Christianity and Islam - was established when God created the heavens and ordered the earth in the story of Genesis and in an early example of faith - or lack of it - in governance, records Adam's questioning of God's role and through his disobedience in the garden of Eden, initiated the struggle between good and bad governance. As a consequence of this event the people of God down the ages struggled to fulfil the earlier, but broken, promise of Paradise and, as they did so, a key question arose which was that of the governance of the world's unruly Babel.

Contributing & conflicting models of leadership

One of the many signs of the working out of this struggle was the way that leadership was subsequently interpreted by those responsible for governance and in the Bible the roles that the prophets, kings and priests played in this governance story - each of whom with their distinctive role - still provides rich material for the study of leadership and its varied meanings.

First there were prophets who were self-appointed but claimed a legitimate role in warning and advising the king-governor; sometimes acting as the visionary - the director of scenarios planning in the company - on the inside, but often crying in the wilderness for justice - the campaigning shareholder at the AGM from the outside. This model of leadership reminds us of the importance of non-executive directors and of the role that they have to question the board diligently from an outsider's perspective. For example, Isaiah spoke about God's mercy, or power, being dependent upon obedience but kings and princes thought otherwise when it suited them and responded with: 'Do you think words can take the place of skill and strength?' The arrogant Chair or CEO is a well-recognised figure in the boardroom and as a part of the current debate about governance we have witnessed some of the great corporate moguls seeking to place themselves beyond the scrutiny of others. A recent example has been that of Shell and its leadership's repeated but clumsy attempts to cover up shortcomings in its accounting for its oil reserves.

One problem which often arose was the issue of verification and the question of authenticity, which is also a key area of leadership today: What are the qualities of an authentic leader who will generate trust and confidence so that his or her authority is more than their appointment?

Prophets took their authenticity from a number of sources including their relationship with God Himself and from the people who heard their voices crying in the wilderness and responded to them. Authentic leadership often includes a quality of truth and righteousness, which encourages and compels those who hear to be followers. This has been called the 'charisma' or spirit of the leader. A key aspect of governance and the task of directors are therefore to create a vision for the company or organisation as a whole and to inspire others to 'buy into' it and to be willing to follow.

Vision and buy-in are a part of the director's and the board's role as good stewards. A well ordered board that fulfills its conformance and performance roles with a view to both long and short-term goals is showing leadership. A board that is able to both develop creative strategies at the same time as maintaining its governance roles is showing leadership. The board that is only a 'supra-management committee' is not showing leadership.

Second, there were princes who assumed to themselves by heritage or conquest authority for the activities of the nation on whose behalf they claimed the right to dispense justice and uphold tradition. Sometimes this was welcome and at other times emphatically not. When this was the case, the people would long for a just prince who would save them from tyranny and believed that such an individual would bear God's image. In the same way, the authentic leader legitimises his or her leadership by winning and holding the loyalty and trust of those they lead and good governors maintain this through just decisions, which are understood and trusted by those who they govern.

Third, there were priests, who acted as go-betweens, neither non-executive prophet nor princely CEO. The role of the priest was to maintain the security of the people and keep them safe: Facing towards God in the sacred aspects of the life of the Temple and facing towards the people in pastoring to their everyday needs: Under divine authority on the one hand and under a duty of care on the other. Priests were also the teachers and educators of the nation with a role in meaning-making out of the experiences of life which could be linked to the unlimited possibilities of human life and to creating a vision for the future. In governance, the priest's role was similar to the role of Chair: Not usually working in the company as a full-time executive with day to day responsibility for it, but interpreting its meaning to others both internally through questioning its activities and policies and externally by explaining its merits to its shareholders and stakeholders. There can only be one Chair to each company board, but all directors share the responsibility with the Chair for the development amongst all of them of these three key leadership qualities of prophecy, justice and the go-between.

Discussion points

- Have you a 'prophet' on your board and how do you value his or her contribution and encourage it?
- When was the last time that your board discussed what it means by 'authentic leadership'?
- What steps does your board take to ensure that the loyalty and trust of employees is sustained?
- Can your board identify who are its 'go-betweens' amongst its directors?

The servant leader

For many years, in the search for examples of the quality of character most sought after in leadership, the man Jesus has been used - honoured by both Jews and Muslims as well as by Christians. He was a visionary and weaver of dreams; He spoke as 'One with authority' and he was an accomplished teacher. As a leader with such attributes, He might have been expected to enjoy corporate success but His mission ended instead in apparent failure. An important virtue in leadership is an appreciation of the experience of failure as redemptive and the place for learning. For example, General Dwight Eisenhower had two speeches prepared on the eve of the invasion of Normandy planned for the 6th June 1944, one announcing success and the other the failure of the D-Day landings and many leaders have attested to the positive role that earlier failures have played in their careers and the learning that they have experienced through transcending adversity before becoming successful at their third or fourth attempt at leading a company or organisation.

In his book 'The Leadership of Jesus', John Adair highlights a number of attributes which he believes contributed to the formation of Jesus' leadership qualities which included: His life story drawn from His experience, His membership and use of a team who He was able to inspire, His vision for human beings and the world which He called the 'Kingdom' - His model for good governance - and His humility in the face of those to whom He listened. This last feature, the humility of the listener, has contributed to the model of the servant-leader with which Jesus is particularly associated with its idea of 'The first shall be last and the last, first'. (**Adair, J.**) Qualities of leadership can also be about being available for others, affirming the skills and contribution of others, meeting the needs of others and the sharing of hardship with others.

In her book 'Rewiring the Corporate Brain' Danah Zohar describes the four essential qualities of the servant leader: *"They must have a deep sense of the interconnectedness of life and all its enterprises. They must have a sense of engagement and responsibility, a sense of 'I have to'. They must be aware that all human endeavours, including business, are part of the larger and richer fabric of the whole universe. And perhaps most important of all, servant leaders must know what they ultimately serve. They must, with a sense of humility and gratitude, have a sense of the source from which all values emerge."* She concludes: *"To these servant leaders and others like them, the business of business no longer restricts itself to manipulating things and nature and people for-profit. Rather, business becomes a spiritual vocation in the largest sense of the word.....I believe that it is only from such a basis of spiritual servant leadership that really deep transformation can come about in the corporate world."* (**Zohar, D.**)

All such attributes can contribute to the formation of authentic leadership and become part of meaning-making in power and authority which can subsequently be accepted by others and which can enable leaders and those with responsibilities for governance to become even more effective.

Authentic leadership

There have been many examples of societies - both secular and religious - supposedly modeling themselves upon great religious leaders and the early Christian Church was one such which tried to put the virtues that Jesus' kingdom represented into practice after His death. The main governance responsibility that these Christian leaders believed was that they had to be the faithful carriers of the 'tradition' of the teaching of Jesus about the Kingdom through the education of His followers - the corporate story!

This, they believed, needed to be accompanied by their blameless conduct within the community which quality they would receive as a gift of the Spirit through the laying on of hands. To manage the work of the new Church, such individuals were appointed by the community to leadership roles as 'overseers' of their congregations, with 'deacons' responsible for the organisation and management of the community's social and pastoral activities. The authenticity of these individual leaders came not only from the conviction that they were directed and guided by the Spirit which they had received, but also through the authenticating of its reception by the community which accepted their leadership role.

One of the enduring tasks of the Church therefore became the discernment of the vocation of its leaders and ways to authenticate it, which remains one of the key tasks of governance today in the way that leaders are identified and developed at work. Thus larger companies appoint senior executives to be responsible for leadership; organise programmes for leadership development designed to discern leadership potential, teach leadership skills and engage headhunting firms to search for candidates with qualities who could act as their non-executive directors. Whilst it is generally agreed that Jesus did not lay down any specific instructions about how His successors might order themselves, the attributes He promoted were incorporated into the Church in the same way that the articulation and promotion of a set of company 'values' are part of a company's governance.

Soon, however, a more hierarchical leadership model of the Church emerged and one of the best known of the early fathers, Bishop Ignatius (AD108) described his own governance role as: 'We must regard the bishop as Lord himself'. This was the start of a spiral that led to the church taking up dictatorial positions on many of the key political and social issues of the day and which was to lead eventually to the violent revolutions of the Reformation. These attitudes are mirrored in the behaviour of some corporations: 'There is only one way to do it and that's our way!' and it was such behaviour by the Chair of Marks & Spencer, Sir Richard Greenbury over many years - and without the independent and non-executive directors asserting their roles - that the company's share value was destroyed.

Regressive leadership

The Church rapidly regressed in the way it organised itself away from its initial horizontal, responsive and collective model back to the model of the prince's more hierarchical leadership role of the Old Testament. Whilst reforms were initiated at various times, the church became associated with that of a centralised regime under a uniform system of canon law. These developments were not unlike the pressures that have been placed upon directors by the introduction of codes of conduct designed to deal with the worst of the excesses in a very few boardrooms.

There is now a danger that the active director acutely aware of all of the issues associated with his or her role could be replaced by individuals adhering to a rigid set of codes of conduct instead of using their skills, knowledge and experience to take decisions made in faithfulness. This development would remove the historic 'fiduciary' duty from the role - which is the foundation of each director's purpose - in favour of anonymous regulatory bodies populated by individuals with little front-line experience of being a director reinforced by a 'box ticking' mentality of bureaucracy. This would turn every aspect of governance into an issue of obedience through compliance with regulations that would have the effect of substituting a governance process of reflection, education and learning into one in which the attributes of external command and control would be dominant.

This would lead to a situation where those who disagreed with the codes would at best be banned from acting as a director and at worst be persecuted. There are already signs that some of our most talented younger directors who would formerly be expected to join large corporations in the publicly quoted sector as their career choice are instead joining private equity capital firms in order to avoid further entanglement with the current drive into codes.

Discussion points

- Does your board spend time learning lessons from failure whilst not spending time apportioning blame?

- Does your board spend time discussing the principles, style and attributes of leadership it expects of itself and applies in the company?

- Does your board have ways to appraise the effect its leadership style has upon others and is able to curb any excesses it uncovers?

Visionary leadership

Here again history provides contrasting models of leadership one of which is about rights and the other about responsibilities. Power and authority make life difficult for truth and directors are often driven to select one or the other model rather than struggle to maintain some kind of balance between the two.

Experience shows that such hierarchical organisational structures which are more about obedience than participation are unlikely to: *'Build an organisation where it is safe for people to create visions, where inquiry and truth are the norms and where challenging the status quo is expected'* (**Senge, P.**). The foundational story of the Fall is still topical when those in governance are tempted to serve their own needs first and ignore the rights of others as the 'Fat Cat' scandals have shown. Good Governance is therefore about achieving the highest standards with regards to the best behaviours of which human beings are capable, whilst acknowledging the need for safeguards to give protection from the worst.

The very human tendency towards the seduction of absolute power, authority, command and control as acceptable leadership method is in sharp contrast to the more consultative and communicative style which Jesus practiced which has become usual in the post-modern era. However, one management guru has remarked: 'Command and control is still the driving force behind many organisations and the inclusive and consensual approach is a public relations illusion. It often masks the nefarious activities of a single dominant player at the top who scares the wits out of everyone around him. All the (corporate) disasters of the past 10 years had not one consensual board of directors between them.'

From the above, one puzzling aspect of governance is the way that some leaders whilst claiming to practice an inclusive and democratic approach, actually dominate their board of directors in ways that prevent good governance from flourishing. If people will only trust those who understand them, qualities such as encouragement, involvement, commitment and honesty will be needed to fulfil the needs of good governance and leaders will spend time and effort practising these attributes and achieving recognition from those they lead. Such attributes are important to the development of good governance, but the way they are felt - the quality of governance that is experienced by those exposed to it - in reality often varies greatly and this can produce tensions which can lead to disruption and dissent amongst owners and other stakeholders, especially staff.

Creative leadership

Senge's alternative leadership style, which he calls 'Personal Mastery', is based upon a creative spirit which he believes goes beyond competency and skills. For him, the vision that comes from the leader is a vocation rather than 'simply a good idea' and that this vocation encourages the commitment of others: That practicing the virtues of a fulfilling life and achieving organisational success are not only compatible but enrich one another: A far cry from the traditional attitude towards the iniquities of the market place or the supposedly superior life in the public or community services!

Recently there has also been an increasing focus upon the key role of not just the individual leader as a learner and teacher but also upon the development of the learning organisation in which all the company's employees are set. The reflective practice of the leader, which is the mark of the true professional, and which can also become a key attribute for organisational success, is about the leader's role to encourage and challenge as a way to promote change which in turn can help to create and foster trust and confidence by valuing skills and competencies.

Other trust-building activities include building community, encouraging open communication and telling the truth so that at the heart of the relationship between the leaders and the led is the trust which gives to these other individuals the faith-in-leader which will inspire them to follow him or her. This trust works in both directions so that whilst the leader can take decisions, he or she allows others to do so as well: The leader does not so much exercise power alone, but empowers others to exercise their gifts in their own vocations.

Leadership as learning

The key characteristic of this model of leadership - which is that of the learner-leader and reflective practitioner - is linked to the creation of an authentic power and authority in governance which has less to do with hierarchy and more to do with ideas because: 'Authority is essentially bound up with systems of ideas (which have meaning) and systems of ideas essentially involve the possibility of discussion and criticism.' This emphasis upon governance as learning and educating and as an intellectual activity of reasoning, knowing and thinking, which was also John Lilburne's model for the democratic debates on Putney Common, is in sharp contrast to governance as hierarchy and control with its emphasis upon status that was the tradition of kings and church. This enlightened model of leadership calls upon those who govern to be open, inquiring and committed to the potential that others have for personal development so that an important role of governance is to instruct, train and communicate.

Examples which emphasise this learning approach to governance focus upon authority and governance as a continuing process of discernment and response in which leadership and its attendant skills are expressed and applied.

The key processes to achieve this include teaching and learning and whilst the threat of coercion through the use of power may ensure obedience, the bearer of authority - who is the leader - needs to be seen as trustworthy through their demonstrable competency in their role. Such authority in leadership is made authentic through learning: An individual both fit to act as a governor by setting an example by being a learner and trainer him or herself and one who helps others to govern fitly as learners and trainers in their own turn.

Faithful leadership

In a later book, 'Faithful Change', Fowler uses the story of the ordering of creation to demonstrate not only the use of power and authority to structure the universe in its rightful order but also to promote the conditions of trust, loyalty, mutual regard and sensitivity which are amongst the essential attributes needed for humans to flourish. Fowler believes that deep in the creative and evolutionary process such structures exist and that humans flout them at their peril and claims that these structures need to be recovered and reflected upon to give them new meaning. The post-modern era calls therefore for a balanced perspective upon the need for continued vigilance against oppression - caused by the selfish use of power and authority - as well as affirming the basic virtues of the common good - the virtues of good governance. (**Fowler, J.W.**)

Questions for corporate governors

The leadership of the board

☐ What is your model of leadership?

☐ Is the model of leadership of the CEO consistent with what your board is trying to achieve?

☐ Does the chairman lead the board?

☐ Does the board have a working constitution?

☐ Does the board have a list of reserved powers?

☐ How is the board and its sub-committees structured?

☐ How clearly is the role of CEO and Chairman delineated and defined?

☐ Does the board have written job description for individual members?

☐ Does the board induct newly appointed board members?

☐ Does the board have an annual schedule of meetings, determined a year in advance?

☐ Does the board circulate clear and thorough board papers, including an agenda, to all members two to three weeks before each meeting?

☐ Does the board maintain complete and accurate minutes of all meetings?

☐ Does the Chairman keep meetings brief and well focused and stimulate the broadest possible participation by members?

☐ Does each board member serve on at least one board committee?

Table 8.1 *The leadership of the board*

Conclusion

Leadership and its meanings evolve continually and today's corporate hero is often tomorrow's fallen idol. A number of the examples of leadership with which we are familiar are associated with the 'authoritarian' model and those that reflect the servant-leader are less common. Leadership styles will change as circumstances, often outside of the control of the individual director or of the board, change. What matters are that directors and boards spend time reflecting upon their individual and corporate leadership style and ask themselves if it is appropriate for the company's present situation.

Such reflection can form the basis for the development of new language to describe he leadership that is needed for sustainable success and at the same time describe the vocation of leadership which is located at that point of interchange between vigilance and virtue, between power and submission and between prophetic wisdom and engaging with people.

CHAPTER NINE - GOVERNANCE AS EDUCATION & LEARNING

- How can directors help themselves to perform even better in their roles and responsibilities?

- How can the governance agenda become part of every discussion at the board?

- How can the virtues of good governance be passed on to staff and to all those associated with the company?

- How can even 'top dog' directors learn more about the way the world is, the forces that shape it and how it really works?

- Appointment to the position of director is the beginning of a new era of training and development and not the end of it.

As we have noted in chapters 7 and 8 - Power and Authority in Governance and Leadership in Governance - governance can be spoken of in many different ways including: Governance as power, authority and obedience; as duty, service and representative; as consultative, communicative and confidence-building and as assenting, communitarian and open. Another definition is that of governance as revealing, explanatory and being available to others with its associated qualities of education and learning.

To *reveal* means that governance is an art; that there are principles to be learned and that these can be mastered.

To *explain* means that there is willingness towards openness by the listener; that reflection will lead to deeper knowledge and that from this process better governance will grow.

To *be available* means that those who govern will be present in the places where those who are governed can be found; that through this presence the understanding of the attributes of good governance can be shared and that greater knowledge can lead to greater skills in their application.

Nicholas Lash proposed four ways to understand governance as learning. (**Lash, N.**) These were:

Governance as school

This is about having a thorough grounding in the key attributes of good governance, which can help to make the individual governor credible and authentic to and for others. One example of the way this grounding can occur has been the introduction of the world's first ever qualification that recognises the capabilities of a director - the IoD's Chartered Director Award - which has been designed to make credible and authenticate the learning and practice that an individual has achieved and confirms the idea of governance as 'school'. An individual who has spent time and effort developing their understanding of good governance will reflect their knowledge in everything they do and developing governance as an educational project will identify learners, teachers and areas of study or 'disciplines' which can form parts of the educational process and resource. When people are learning about governance they should feel that they are participating in a precious human activity.

Governance as understanding

This is about understanding the complexities of the governance role which includes the attributes referred to earlier which are about the qualities of leadership and the use of power and authority that good governance demands. For example, reference was made to the qualities of secular leaders who commanded respect, to the prophets, kings and priests of the old era and of Jesus in the new era, and how some of their good attributes can help to build up an understanding of the overall governance role. Amongst these qualities are: Legitimacy, vision, authenticity, truthfulness, righteousness, tradition, loyalty, trustfulness, humility and an awareness of the possibility of failure. The good governor holds all these attributes in balance to develop his or her governance role, which has the well being of the corporation and its stakeholders at its centre.

Governance as teaching

Lash writes how teaching leads to learning of which three questions will be asked: What to teach, how to teach it and why should it be taught? The late Cardinal Basil Hume quoting Thomas Aquinas wrote: 'I recognise the duty to teach and guide but that an appeal to obedience alone is unsatisfactory. St Thomas wrote that we should instruct those who are listening so that they will be brought to an understanding of the truth envisaged. Here, one must rely on arguments, which probe the root of truth and make people know how what is said is true. Otherwise, the hearer will acquire no knowledge or understanding but will go empty away'.

Good governance is about truth and goes to the heart of what life is about. The teaching of governance is not therefore about one part of life, divorced from other aspects of who we are, it is about the whole of life itself.

Unfortunately few boardroom practitioners have the time, inclination or skills to teach their art to a wider audience and even fewer universities or colleges offer courses related to boardroom practice. This can add to feelings of mistrust about what directors actually do with their time at the board and lead to further isolation in the boardroom: Corporate citadels under siege from regulators are unlikely to be the best place for individuals to learn, for example, the differences between governing and managing

Governance as culture

Leaders may yearn for a different time, for example, a time when orders given by those in responsibility were not questioned by those to whom they were given to carry out. Such ideas cannot be applied in our time as we live in a culture in which, for example, through education, access to information and the suspicion of leaders, continual questioning is the norm. If governance is to be learned, those who teach it must first understand the world in which they live. It is not a requirement that they should necessarily agree or disagree, approve or disapprove of what goes on in the world, but they need to understand and understanding requires attentiveness and sympathy with the concerns of contemporary culture and of the world as it is.

Governance as explanation

Whereas a standard account of the dawning of modernity through the age of The Enlightenment may have seen rationality and science banishing superstition, post-modernity acknowledges the confusion and diversity which continuing and rapid change brings. Governance has no final answers but is an aspect of learning which tries to bring a measure of clarity to complex issues of human life.

The principles described above are about the need for a commitment to truth and to an understanding of the structures underlying current events. Once such structures have been recognised it is a key task of leadership to free individuals from the mysterious forces that dictate their behaviour - and which can so often produce negative results or bad governance - so that governance can become about educating people to see the truth.

This will only happen if the leader and the organisation which he or she leads becomes a learning organisation of which the key attribute is that of reflective learning and practice. The art of leading is therefore reflection in action which includes the ability not only to cope with, but also to: 'Interpret uncertainty, change and uniqueness (**Schon, D.**)

Learning needs vision and it is the leader and those with responsibility for governance who supply this vision so that new assumptions and new values are identified; new codes of behaviour are introduced and new ways of speaking are learned. The leaders-in-governance who are also reflective-in-action can give meaning to organisational events; can draw upon organisational knowledge and can act as agents for organisational learning so that the store of knowledge is always expanding. These attributes mark a learning organisation and can be used to predict its long-term success. The Centre for Tomorrow's Company in London has used similar indicators to show that when boards of directors attend to the interests of stakeholders, sustainable growth can also be secured.

Discussion points

• How much of your board's time is spent on: 'reporting' compared with 'learning' such as re-examining ideas, innovative thinking, identifying major new concerns and stretching its knowledge?

• Does your board take care of your learning needs and dedicate resources to them?

• Does you board organise 'away days' or special board meetings or Agenda items about its progress towards becoming a 'learning organisation' and how often does it measure the volume and depth of learning going on in the company?

The Learning Organisation

In his book 'The Learning Organisation & the need for directors who think' (**Garratt, B.**), Bob Garratt lists amongst the necessary characteristics of directors the need to manage boundaries, to take an integrative view, to coach other staff, to broaden horizons and to make time to think and Peter Schwartz adds to these: Thinking about issues, re-examining ideas, identifying major concerns, stretching networks and thinking of new scenarios, all of which activities involve learning. (**Schwartz, P.**) A key question for Boards of directors will be the attention they give to such issues, the amount of time they spend discussing them and the effort they make to implement their conclusions.

Whilst the aspiring director - many of whom we meet in the course of our work - represent willing learners who will go on to become good governors, there are still those who feel that by their selection and appointment as a director and by the experience which their career record confirms, that their skills in governance can be assumed. This may have been the case in an earlier age of either less complexity or the sense that those who governed must by definition also have been those who were most suited to their roles by birth or education.

This is clearly no longer the case as governance has become not only a matter for us all; as members of a society in which good governance matters greatly to each one of us as owners, shareholder-pensioners and stakeholders in the provision of public and community services but also a vocation to be learned and mastered by those who exercise it on our behalf like any other profession which demands learning and skill. Until the recent introduction of the qualification of Chartered director pioneered by the Institute of Directors, becoming a director required no prior knowledge whatsoever and no commitment to learning.

Questions for corporate governors

Opportunities for learning and improvement

☐ Is the board satisfied with its performance?

☐ What other boards do you have experience serving on?

☐ Are you satisfied with your individual contribution?

☐ What training and development have you undertaken within the last 12 months?

☐ How is board performance evaluated?

☐ Is this evaluation honest and open?

☐ How can it be improved?

☐ What is your training and development plan over the next 12 months?

Table 9.1 Opportunities for learning and improvement

Some questions for the trustee/director in the Third Sector organisation

☐ Can l contribute the necessary time to be an effective board member?

☐ Am l fully appraised of the mission of the organization?

☐ What do l plan to learn from this appointment?

☐ What am l able to contribute in terms of contacts, fund-raising etc?

Table 9.2 Some questions for the Trustee/Director in the Third Sector organisation

Conclusion

Governance as learning is not something that is associated immediately with boards of directors in the way that power, authority and leadership might be expected as attributes. There is an assumption too that by the time an individual has sufficient experience for appointment to the board, that his or her learning is complete. However, it would be hard to find a director who in their career up to joining a board has had exposure to this field of study and the learning needed within it. Issues of knowledge, of contemporary culture and an appreciation of the virtues of honesty and trust need to be learned as well as experienced. Governance as learning provides the basis for instruction, for understanding and for practice that no other area of corporate life can offer. Directors who are also learners are directors who survive and grow in stature, strength and achievement.

CHAPTER TEN - THE BOARD: ITS BEHAVIOUR AND CONDUCT

- Governance involves handling risk, crisis, corporate dilemmas and ensuring continuing solvency

- There is a premium to be placed on plain speaking and honesty - directors should use these in the boardroom

- Building candid relationships enables a board to cope with the crises which inevitably occur within and outside the boardroom

- "Effective boards depend as much on behaviours and relationships as on procedures and structures" (Higgs, 2003)

- Governance is about having in place the checks and balances which prevent abuses of power

Corporate governance is not just about rules, codes and regulation, it is about the way directors work and interact together especially in a crisis. A crisis can take many forms - a fatal accident in the factory; a solvency crisis; a strike; an investigation by the DTI; a takeover bid. This is when directors, their faith in each other and in board governance itself are put to the test. In this chapter the social dimension of how a group of directors behave, take decisions and act upon them is explored. Perhaps the real test of a board's resilience in governance is how its members react under pressure and in a crisis.

Well planned governance procedures can help to reduce the 'downside' of a crisis and planning can include how roles are allocated and how the board delegates its overall responsibility to its sub-committees and to management. The architecture of governance helps in a crisis but inevitably it is in the fundamentals of honesty, transparency, good faith and trust within 'right relationships' that enables a board to surmount a crisis.

Nurturing board relationships

"Is there a difference between a man who thinks honesty is the best policy and an honest man?" (C. S. Lewis)

On the face of it Enron operated according to good governance principles and independent non-executive directors, codes of ethics and regular board meetings were all in place. As Jeffrey Sonnenfeld pointed out: *"Despite Enron's disastrously complex financial schemes, no corporation could have had more appropriate financial competencies and experience on its board. The list includes a former Stanford dean who is an accounting professor, the former CEO of an insurance company, the former CEO of an international bank, a hedge fund manager, a prominent Asian financier, and an economist who is the former head of the US government's Commodity Futures Trading Commission!"* (**Sonnenfeld, J.**); but he goes onto suggest that: *"What distinguishes exemplary boards is that they are robust, effective social systems....the key is not structural it is social"*.

The principle of putting others before self provides one key to building 'right relationship'. Despite differences, individuals are bound together: 'No man is an island, entire of himself, every man is a part of the Main' (John Donne). Despite the differences between people and the struggles in which they inevitably engage, individuals are invited to: 'Do unto others as we would have done unto ourselves'. There can be no place for grudges or vendettas in the boardroom as this distorts behaviours, judgement and right relationship.

Bob Tricker describes a number of board styles which are about achieving a balance between the board's governance tasks as well as a concern for the board's relationships. A high performing board is one which is strong on both its concern for board relationships and its concern for the tasks it must perform. In Tricker's model the 'Country Club' board concentrates more upon relationships than it does on getting things done, whilst the 'Rubber Stamp' board can be typical of many SMEs and subsidiary boards who rubber stamp the decisions made by owners higher up in the hierarchy. 'Representative' boards are typical of venture capital funded companies which can become dominated by nominee directors whose main focus is getting the business done. The 'Professional' board, however, has a high concern for both its relationships and its tasks. (**Tricker, R.**)

Board business

"Like the parent of the two year old the board knows it has power but never truly feels in charge."

The average board meets between 10 and 12 times per year and devotes between 3 and 4 hours on board business. The diligent board will ensure that these dates are put into the diary a year ahead so that attendance is 100%. With only 30 to 48 available hours it is important that sub-committees are formed with delegated authority - although responsibility still lies with the full board and that the board is clear about the power it reserves for itself and does not delegate beyond itself. Unlike managers, board members are, of necessity, 'episodic' decision-makers. To avoid confusion and overlap with their full time executives, it will be important that the board spells out the decisions that are reserved for it and those that it agrees should be delegated. Examples of reserved powers can include capital expenditure above an agreed level, statements to the Press, senior management salaries and benefits, acquisitions and disposals, etc.

The Audit and Remuneration sub-committees are a requirement of the Combined Code. The Code states that -

"The board should establish formal and transparent arrangements for considering how they should apply the financial reporting and internal control principles and for maintaining an appropriate relationship with the company's auditors."

It is unwise for directors to 'mark their own exam papers' and non-executive directors should lead a transparent and formal process for deciding on the remuneration package of executive directors.

The audit and remuneration sub committees may be supplemented by other committees such as Environmental, IT, Health and Safety, Nomination, Corporate Governance, etc. It all depends on the circumstances of the company and the work load of the board. This is certainly a way of getting non-executive directors involved - and a good way of building team-work and relationships.

Much of the way a board works will depend on the skill of the Chair to lead and guide the business of the board. The Chair is not Chair of the company but of the board and is the guardian of what the board does and responsible for the integrity of its governing process. The task of the Chair is to encourage the emergence of divergent views and full debate that will over time become the unitary position of the board as a whole. Good governance is not about managing a 'smooth' board room process but is about meetings that are full of argument, disagreement, passion and dissent which are all signs of a healthy board!. The chair is the servant-leader of the board and as first among equals it is the chair that guides the governance process and ensures integrity within it.

Board style matrix

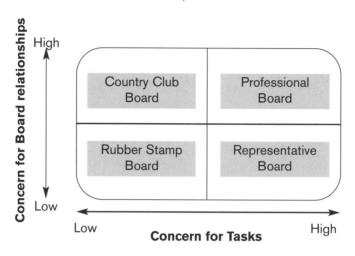

figure 10.1 Board style matrix

Discussion points

*   Where does your board fit on this matrix?
*   How do you develop a concern for relationships on your board?
*   How do you ensure you get the right balance of focus and activity?
*   What are the blockages to candid relationships on your board?

Sonnenfeld describes a 'virtuous circle' of respect, trust and candour amongst a board of directors: *"They seem to get into a virtuous circle in which one good quality builds on another. Team members develop mutual respect; because they respect one another, they develop trust; because they trust one another, they share difficult information; because they all have the same, reasonably complete information, they can challenge one another's conclusions coherently; because a spirited give-and-take becomes the norm, they learn to adjust their interpretations in response to intelligent questions."* (**Sonnenfeld, J.**)

The virtuous circle of the board

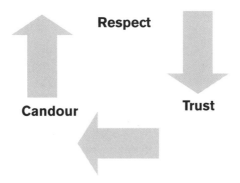

figure 10.2 The virtuous circle of the board

One mark of a board which is serious about building candid board relationships can be seen in the way it inducts new board members whether from within management or from outside the company. Effective induction programmes enable directors to be included more rapidly so that they are able to make an early contribution to the group dynamics of the board. Figure 10.3 charts the level of impact over time. The earlier directors are helped to be able to reach their full potential and develop in their roles, the quicker they will be able to make an impact as effective governors. However, the diagram assumes that over time the impact of a director will inevitably decline and that there will come a time when it will be appropriate for the directors to move on to a new challenge. Under normal circumstances, the period of appointment for a non-executive director would be expected to be a maximum of three terms of 3 years each.

One of the most important governance issues within Third Sector boards is whether the chief executive should be an ex officio member of the board. Although this enhances the authority of the chief executive and strengthens his or her working relationship with the board it can make it difficult for the board to assess the CEO's performance in an open and candid fashion. If they are appointed it is wise to have a regular agenda item which is for the non-executive directors only.

There should be a natural tension between non-executive and executive directors that should be openly acknowledged which is all part of the process of balancing the power and authority of individuals and of the board as a whole. It would be unwise for non-executives to accept at face value everything which is presented by the full time executives. It is the clear duty of a non-executive to have the role to investigate, to 'police' and to probe their actions and this is the task of the independent director. This is one reason that boards which have only full time executives appointed to them are unhealthy boards and can lead to 'rubber stamping' rather than to good and effective governance. The current codes of conduct for directors recommend that at least half of the board should be composed of non-executive directors.

Impact of directors

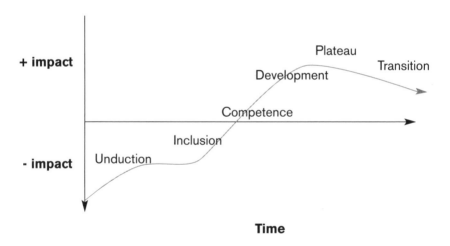

figure 10.3 The Impact of directors

Handling risk and crisis

A fundamental aspect of the role of the board and individual directors is to safeguard the interests of the owners and the company's assets. One of the principles of the Combined Code is: "The board should maintain a sound system of internal control to safeguard shareholders' investment and the company's assets."

The Turnbull report, published in September 1999, provided guidance on the implementation of the internal control requirements of the Combined Code. The report, 'Internal Control: Guidance for Directors on the Combined Code', has the support and endorsement of the London Stock Exchange. Nevertheless, it has useful implications for organizations of all sizes seeking to benefit from more robust risk management systems. In addition, the boards of NHS Trusts, Further Education Colleges and registered charities falling under the supervision of the Charity Commission are all required to make statements about their internal controls and risk management procedures.

Case Study - Lothian Electronics

Lothian Electronics is a small, engineering sub-contractor to Scotland's 'Silicon Glen'. They supply mission critical, machined parts and their customer base includes some of the top global names in electronics and telecommunications. Because the manufacturing plant is on the flight path into Edinburgh airport there is a requirement for a disaster recovery plan.

Discussion points

* What key elements should the board take into account in developing a disaster recovery plan?

* What did your board learn from the Y2K planning exercise and cyber attacks through the Internet since then?

* What lessons on business continuity did your board take from the disaster of 9/11?

* Use the matrix shown at figure 10.4 below to map out the scale of risk confronting your company

* What kind of potential risks and disasters would keep you awake at night?

The Turnbull report states that a company's system of internal control: "Has a key role in the management of risks that are significant to the realization of its business objectives" and should be: "Embedded in the operations of the company and form part of its culture". The report recommends that the board focuses on the full range of risks facing the company, including: "Health, safety and environmental, reputation and business probity issues."

A genuine concern for the health and safety of employees is a basic governance duty and should not be turned into a 'box ticking' exercise to protect board members from litigation under the Health and Safety Act. There have been a number of recent examples in which boards have been unaware of unsafe working practices being carried out in their name and under their very noses. The way a company impacts on its environment is rightly heavily regulated and controlled so that the natural environment is conserved and the company that pollutes becomes socially unacceptable.

The Report also states that a company's system of day-to-day controls should be embedded in its operations and culture rather than being an 'add on' function. It should also be capable of responding quickly to evolving risks, whether arising inside the company or in the business environment. Businesses should not look upon such guidance as a regulatory burden only; internal control frameworks can increase shareholder value and come to represent best practice for directors. Indeed, evaluating and controlling risks on a systematic basis can lead to:

* Opportunities not being lost
* Competitive advantage
* High value 'strategic thinking'
* Less management time in fire-fighting

The report, Internal Control: Guidance for Directors on the Combined Code (**The Turnbull report**), is available from the web-site of the Institute of Chartered Accountants in England and Wales (ICAEW): www.icaew.co.uk/internalcontrol

Managing Risk

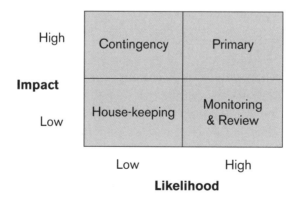

figure 10.4 *Managing Risk*

Getting to grips with insolvency

All organizations can fail and become insolvent i.e. the company does not have the cash resources to meet liabilities as they become due for payment. As part of their duty of care, directors need to understand the financial health of their company; this cannot be delegated to the financially skilled or aware directors only. Wrongful trading may be broadly defined as a failure by a director of a company to take every step that he or she should have taken to minimise loss to creditors once he or she knew or ought to have known that the company was unlikely to avoid insolvent liquidation.

This can be a real dilemma for directors and is a difficult call to make - in short it can become the sternest test of a director's stewardship. Winding up a company is rarely in the interests of its owners and there is often the temptation to try and trade through a cash crisis. The process calls for plain speaking and an honest assessment of the situation. Too often boards are plagued with 'corporate speak' which encourages a positive 'spin'; a problem is never termed a problem but an opportunity, or at worst a challenge. This can be misleading and downright dangerous in a time of real crisis. Once the Rubicon has been crossed into insolvency then the duties of the director are to serve the interests of creditors. Creditors can, in the case of a company in liquidation, apply to the court for an order compelling the directors to repay such sum as the court considers just in respect of the directors' 'misfeasance or breach of trust'.

Tests of insolvency

There are a number of ways to test for insolvency and every industry, business and organization will apply their own key measures. At the very least directors must be able to understand the Cash Flow, Balance Sheet and cash position of their company. Around 23% of company directors experience company failure through insolvency and some 7% experience multiple failures. There are some obvious warning signs;

Warning	Signs
Failure to comply with loan covenants	High borrowings
Falling liquidity	Weak investment decision-making
Large contingent liabilities	Dominant customer(s)
PAYE & NI in arrears	Sharp rise in overheads
Bad debts looming	Lack of rigour in debt collection
Weakening margins	Declining stock turn ratios
Qualified audit reports	Capital base too small
Incomplete management accounts	Over-dependence on FD
Failure to address situation	Hiding from creditors

Table 10.5 Warning signs

Apart from these warning signs directors should also consider the following:

- Is the company paying its bills for materials, services, rent etc as they fall due or shortly thereafter, and can it continue to do so in the foreseeable future?

- Do the aggregate liabilities, including contingent or prospective liabilities, exceed the total value of the company's assets?

- If the company were put into liquidation today would the money realized from the disposal of the assets be sufficient to pay all liabilities and the costs of the liquidation in full?

- Obtains proper professional advice on all material matters not within the general knowledge, skill, and experience of the company's own directors and senior staff

Balance of power on the board

We have already explored the balance of power which exists between the owner-shareholders, the company's board and the management. We now turn to the principle of the balancing of these interests within the boardroom.

A requisite of good governance is that power is not abused. A dangerous phenomenon is what happens when a board is dominated by a single individual through ownership or sheer force of personality. One of the most notorious examples of abuse of power was the story of Lonhro and its leader the 'charismatic' 'Tiny' Rowland. Rowland first turned the sleepy London and Rhodesian Mining and Land into the formidable global company Lonrho and in the process provided high returns for shareholders. He was an autocrat and moved around Africa completing deals with African leaders including Nkomo, Nyerere and Kaunda and then began to build his business in Europe along similar lines. He was a 'swashbuckling' entrepreneur who had no time for the formalities of governance or transparency. In 1973 fellow director Sir Basil Smallpiece led a board rebellion against 'Tiny' Rowland's leadership. He was supported by the then Prime Minister Edward Heath who described Lonrho as the "unpleasant and unacceptable face of capitalism" but at an Exceptional General Meeting of owner-shareholders these rebel directors were removed and the board was returned to 'Tiny's' control.

Another example is that of Lord Black, the former chairman of Hollinger International (HI), who, it was claimed in a US court recently, routinely tried to intimidate other directors and even threatened to sue them if they stood in his way! The late Giovanni Angelli, of the founding Fiat family, was reputed to have said: "Only an odd number of directors can run a company, and three is too many" whilst Sam Goldwyn typified the attitude of many of the 'baron's of industry when he remarked to a subordinate "I want you to tell me what you think, even if it costs you your job!".

Any concentration of power in the boardroom is unhealthy. Directors are collectively responsible for any board decisions and should express their own judgement and interpretation of what is in the best interests of the company, rather than being mere 'yes' men or women. There are 3 key principles of corporate governance in the UK that are designed to ensure a healthy balance of power.

1. **The separation of the roles of CEO and Chairman.**

    The Combined Code states that: "There are two key tasks at the top of every public company - the running of the board and the executive responsibility for the running of the company's business. There should be a clear division of responsibilities at the head of the company which will ensure a balance of power and authority such that no one individual has unfettered powers of decision." The Code also specifies that a CEO should not go on to become chairman of the same company.

2. **The introduction of non-executive directors.**

    The Code also recommends that: "The board should include a balance of executive and non-executive directors (including independent non-executives) such that no individual or small group of individuals can dominate the board's decision taking."

3. **Appointments to the board**

    The Code states that: "There should be a formal, rigorous and transparent procedure for the appointment of new directors to the board." All public companies are encouraged to have a nominations committee reporting to the board which consists of a majority of independent non-executive directors.

Case Study - Pinson Foods

You have recently been appointed as a Non-executive Director to a £50m turnover, privately-owned food processing business. You were school-chums with the Chairman/CEO and majority shareholder; you are delighted with the £10k fees the appointment pays. The Accounts show that Board remuneration has increased 60% over the last 3 years whilst profit margins have been static. Shop-floor pay has increased 7.5% over the same period. The company is embarking on a policy of TQM and improved communications with the 600 workforce on 4 sites as part of a strategy to increase margins and break-out of the squeeze exerted by the retail multiples. This is of such critical importance that a board sub-committee has been set up to monitor the TQM project and, in the Chairman's words, "to help you get your feet under the table I want you to chair this sub-committee." An employee survey, which forms part of the TQM project, indicated a distinct lack of shop-floor morale and a number of 'digs' about the 'flashy' Directors cars and 'opulent' new Boardroom. You believe that the Board should have some policy on remuneration along the lines of Cadbury and Greenbury.

More worryingly the Procurement Manager has told you that the Chairman has promised to raise £20k for his favourite charity - The Duke of Cumbernauld Trust - and has asked him to call key vendors and request that each contribute £1k to the cause. "This will demonstrate your commitment to the team and advance your career prospects" are the Chairman's words left ringing in the ears of the Procurement Manager.

Discussion points

- What are the governance issues in the case?
- How will you tackle them at the next board meeting?

Conflicts of interest

Conflicts of interest inevitably arise and can put even the best run boards to the test. Boards within the Third Sector serve the broad public good and when board members fail to exercise reasonable care in their oversight of the organization they are not living up to the trust that the public has placed in them. All board members should fully disclose interests which may be relevant to their role; this can be carried out on an annual basis and in some cases even published within the annual report. Board members who have an actual or potential conflict of interest should not participate in discussion when such interests are discussed or vote on matters affecting transactions between the organization and the conflicting issue, individuals or group. These conflicts can arise through interests individual directors may have in contractors and suppliers businesses or through family members who have interests in these contractors and suppliers.

Conclusion

The architecture of governance is not built up in isolation. It means nothing unless there are candid and open relationships between board members; relationships which foster open dissent, debate and argument. The domination of the board by an individual or cabal is dangerous - a system of checks and balances is needed to ensure sound governance. Although Michael Grade, newly appointed Chairman of the BBC, was reported as saying that: "Non-executive directors are like bidets; they look pretty but nobody is quite sure how to use them", they can play a valuable role in checking the power of the executive directors. The true test of a board comes about when handling risk, crisis and dilemma - the essential components of board decision-making.

CHAPTER 11 - CRISIS, CONSTRAINTS AND CATASTROPHES

"If one were to study all the laws, one would have absolutely no time to break them" (Goethe)

- How should directors deal with laws and regulations that are contrary to natural justice and equity?

- Codes of conduct should help not hinder

- Directors duties in respect of accounts are stringent and comprehensive

- Employment law changes can create mistrust between employers and employees

- Seeking appropriate legal advice is a basic duty of care

- It is prudent to take out directors' liability insurance

- Many trade associations and member organizations provide low cost sources of legal advice and advocacy

There are over 250 laws that carry penalties for directors - some of them incurring prison sentences - and the list keeps growing! This is further evidence of the breakdown in trust between society and the boardroom. To complicate matters further wide ranging changes to Company Law have been proposed by Government which will be introduced when parliamentary time permits. Many directors will throw their arms up in horror and wonder just how they can get to grips with such a volume of legislation encroaching upon, and limiting their activities!

The burden of regulation and red tape consistently comes at the top of all IOD surveys as the most irritating aspect of a director's role and the directors of small firms report that they spend up to a day a week dealing with it. A simple piece of advice is to seek expert help, take out appropriate insurance cover and not let the time spent on these matters impinge on the real added-value role of the director!

Although many of the proposed changes to Company Law are designed to simplify the situation for the smaller concern, there will inevitably be increases in cost and time when new legislation is introduced. Since the current Companies Act does not provide a comprehensive statement of directors' general duties and responsibilities it is helpful to restate the guiding principles for the behaviour of directors.

- Fiduciary duty

Each director must act in accordance with what he or she believes to be in the best interests of the company. Directors must not place themselves in a position in which there is a conflict between their duties to the company and their personal interests.

- Care and skill

The standard of care expected is of: "Such care as an ordinary man or woman might be expected to take on his or her own behalf". The degree of skill expected is of: "such a degree of skill as may reasonably be expected from a person with (the particular directors) knowledge and experience".

To exercise proper fiduciary duty, care and skill will require that a board will seek expert advice to ensure that the company and each individual as stewards are operating within the law. A complete treatment of the law and how it relates to directors is beyond the scope of this book but we have highlighted some key areas that can bring directors into conflict with the law.

Charities and other not-for-profit organisations are regulated in a similar fashion to the business sector: That sufficient information is provided to stakeholders, that accounts are kept, that governance is conducted properly, that the interests of certain stakeholders are considered, and that fraud is prevented. Because of the tax advantages they enjoy, registered charities face a heavier burden of regulation through the Charity Commission than non-charitable, not-for-profit organizations. Company law does not recognise the status of 'trustee', so that in the eyes of this law trustees are directors, although they are all volunteers. For example, the Charity Commission makes it almost impossible to pay trustee-directors but insists on trustees taking full legal responsibility for all the activities of a charity.

Wrongful trading - don't be the last to know

The importance of monitoring solvency has already been mentioned and the Insolvency Act 1986 states that directors may be liable for wrongful trading unless they take all proper steps to minimise the creditors' potential losses, once they know, or ought to conclude, that there is no reasonable prospect that insolvent liquidation can be avoided. The potential penalties for wrongful trading are:

- Liability to make a contribution to the assets of the company in a sum to be decided by the court; this is the main implication of unlimited liability for a director

- Disqualification from being concerned in the management of a company in the future

When a company goes into insolvent liquidation, the liquidator, administrative receiver, administrator or Official Receiver has a duty to send to the Secretary of State at the DTI a report on the conduct of all directors who were in office in the company in the last 3 years of its trading. The Secretary of State then decides whether it is in the public interest to seek a disqualification order against a director. The report will assess -

- Whether the directors took such steps to monitor the company's affairs as would be taken by a reasonably prudent business person

- If they failed to do so, whether they would have recognised the company's insolvency earlier if they had taken such steps

It is therefore essential that the board of directors ensures that appropriate steps are taken on a regular basis to monitor the company's financial position. There are over 12,000 company insolvencies each year, c.1,500 directors are disqualified each year and new proceedings are issued against a further 1,775. **(DTI)**

Fraudulent trading

Honest directors will not find themselves guilty of fraudulent trading, although there continues to be high profile cases of rogue directors who swindle their companies, investors and shareholders. On the 8th June 2004 Carl Cushnie, the CEO and Chairman of Versailles Group plc, was sentenced to six years in prison for defrauding wealthy investors of more than £23m. Interestingly this fraud case echoed the Charitable Corporation case of 1731 when investors appeared to be offered a 'sure-fire' return. **(Myerson, J)**

If a company has already incurred liabilities that it failed to pay when they fell due or shortly thereafter, the board should carefully consider their position and place on record the factors that led them to conclude that any further liabilities incurred would be paid at the proper time before the company obtains any additional credit.

The Charity Commission undertakes the monitoring of all registered charities with an income or expenditure over £10,000 in order to detect fraud and abuse. In addition the auditors of registered charities which are not limited companies have a specific statutory duty to report to the Charity Commission abuse or significant breaches of charity law or regulation.

Disqualification - it can happen!

A disqualification order may be made against a director on the grounds of:

- Responsibility for wrongful or fraudulent trading
- Unfitness to be concerned in the management of a company

A disqualification order may also be made if someone is found guilty of an indictable offence in relation to a company, or is in persistent default of filing requirements under the Companies Act 1985. The Companies Act includes some sixty-nine indictable offences, and there are around fifty separate duties placed on directors with regard to filing, so there is great scope for a director to be guilty of either an indictable offence or persistent default!

Directors' duties in respect of accounts are stringent and comprehensive. Directors are responsible for preparing a profit and loss account and a balance sheet, ensuring that proper accounting records are kept, and taking all possible steps to ensure that the accounts show a true and fair view. This is now reflected in the 'Statement of Directors' Responsibilities', which has to be attached to the statutory financial statements.

Directors are also under a statutory duty to supply auditors with necessary information and explanations. This is the reason for the detailed terms and conditions set out by the Auditor in their 'letters of representation'. Criminal liability can follow if director's 'knowingly or recklessly' make a 'misleading, false or deceptive statement' to the auditors.

A disqualification order can run for a minimum of two to a maximum of fifteen years.

A person who is subject to a disqualification order may not:

- Be a director of a company without leave of the court
- Be concerned or take part in any way in the promotion, formation, or management of a company without leave of the court

Recommended as good governance practice is that every board of directors should:

- Minute precisely the particular responsibilities of each board member
- Ensure that appropriate management information is provided to the board at regular intervals, and that action is taken where needed if this is not forthcoming
- Records at least in outline the information presented to it, any action it resolved to take as a result of receiving or discussing such information, and the director or directors responsible for implementing the action

- Seek proper professional advice on all material matters not within the general knowledge, skill, and experience of the company's own directors and senior staff

Case Study - Sweet-tooth Contract Catering Ltd

Karen Lowe is a successful solicitor. At the age of 35 she joins her cousin's company Sweet-tooth Contract Catering Ltd as a non-executive director. Karen has considerable experience of Company law and has a vast range of contacts within the Manchester area. The MD of the company - Chris Coe - is the majority shareholder and has grown the business to £10m in just 5 years on the back of 'blue chip' accounts and local authority contracts. Karen joins the board as the first NXD alongside 3 executive directors and the MD.

After her first week in post she consults the Company books and minutes and is surprised to find that the annual return is overdue and that no-one appears to have notified Companies House of her appointment. At the first board meeting the following week she gets hold of the management accounts for period 5 of the financial year which has taken 25 days to produce. It does not make good reading. Working capital is being sucked into a new contract for Iko Electronics with 6,000 employees over 12 sites. Staged payments are late and the company appears to be technically insolvent. Karen raises her concerns about liquidity but is afraid to rock the boat too much - after all this is her first board meeting. Chris Coe points out that the 'sick' cash flow and balance sheet is fairly typical for the industry and that he did not get where he is today without taking a few risks.

That night Karen goes through a more complete set of financial records and projections and speaks to Ted Fuller the Financial Controller over the phone. Her conclusion - there is nothing that can halt the company's insolvency; Ted remains in denial; she is determined to tackle the other directors the following morning. To her dismay the Sales Director - Tim Storey - does not have a clue about the figures and just 'prattles' on about his success in winning the latest contract and finds Karen's line of questioning 'disloyal'. She does not fare better with John Luckhurst the Operations Director. "I am paid to staff-up and deliver these demanding contracts; over the last 5 years Chris and the Commercial Director - Bob Scanlon - have looked after the figures."

A week later she manages to see Bob Scanlon. He appears aware of the problem but believes he has 'pulled a rabbit out of the hat'. He waves a bank facility letter under her nose from an obscure bank which gives the company a second line of credit. He needs Karen's signature on the facility letter which is unsecured. Karen does not feel she can sign the letter and a fierce argument ensues. Four weeks later the Company's principal bank calls in its loan, and a receiver is appointed.

Discussion points

*   What is the level of skill expected from Karen?
*   What is the level of skill expected from the other 4 directors?
*   What is the form which must be submitted for Karen?
*   What is the potential liability for the board of directors?

Employment law grip tightens

Because of its complexity and rapidly changing scope Employment law creates problems for board members of all types of organization. Under the Companies Act directors are under a legal duty to have regard to the interests of their employees. A cursory view of the popular Press reveals a variety of bizarre cases coming before Employment Tribunals. Over the last decade applications to tribunals have trebled and now run at over 100,000 per annum. The scales of justice can feel so weighted against employers that many avoid any 'hassle' by settling out of court even though 43% may feel that they might have won their case. (**DTI**)

This trend is likely to continue as new regulations such as the Employment Equality -Sexual Orientation and Religion or Belief (December 2003) are added to the list of over 80 regulations already in force. These latest additions could pose particular problems for directors. It is now illegal to discriminate directly or indirectly against homosexuals, lesbians, transsexuals, and even practicing witches and pagans! Sexual orientation is defined as an orientation towards -

persons of the same sex.

persons of the opposite sex.

persons of the same sex and of the opposite sex.

This legislation is predicted to generate a 'field day' for employment lawyers and considerable expense for employers.

The placing of a job advertisement for a Children's Charity which requests applicants for a maintenance man and cook, and which states, or implies, that a married couple is sought would be deemed to be discriminating against homosexuals. The very term maintenance man may be illegal under the terms of the Sex Discrimination Act! Under Regulation 22 of the Sexual Orientation regulations any harassment carried out by an individual employee will be deemed to be carried out by the employer, whether or not it is done with the employer's knowledge or approval. Employers are therefore obliged to have an Equal Opportunities Policy and a Harassment Policy and to train their staff to avoid liability for the acts of their employees.

Side-stepping the Law

Recent research by the Small Business Council (**The Daily Telegraph**) found that some legislation appeared to influence employers' behaviour negatively, with some firms, run by both men and women, admitting that maternity leave and childcare issues meant they did not employ any women. The respondents said that the employment tribunal system was undermining employer/employee relations, with employers becoming more "wary" of their staff: "*Employers perceive that any employee can instigate a tribunal claim; it costs them nothing and there are no repercussions if the employee fails to attend, whereas the employer would be penalised,*" the report stated. Sarah Anderson, Council member leading on the research, said the message that Government should take, however unpalatable, was that regulation does not work for small firms: "*Officials should be more imaginative about achieving policy objectives rather than seeing regulation as the silver bullet that solves the problem.*"

Rather than embrace the stifling impact of employment regulation many firms are seeking to minimize its impact by reducing their existing policies to the minimum required to avoid claims of discrimination from staff, which could land the firm in an employment tribunal. These are clear examples of the heavy hand of regulation undermining the trust between employer and employee within an organisation that is needed for success and delivering the very opposite of what was intended.

Other legal hurdles

In a recent survey commissioned by the IOD and CMS Cameron McKenna, directors were asked: 'Which areas of law or regulation do you think present the greatest degree of risk of personal liability?' Top of the list was Health and Safety and Product liability law. Mark Tyler of CMS stated in the report: "Directors' perceptions about health and safety risks are spot on. HSE investigations into serious accidents now routinely go right to the top of management structures and look at personal responsibilities. The forthcoming Corporate Killing legislation will focus attention more than ever on high level management control." (**IOD/CMS**)

Once in place, the new law will even allow road fatalities to be viewed as a crime; which means that a company or a director may be held 'vicariously' liable for a death due to 'management failure'. It will be the responsibility of directors to ensure that any company cars or private cars used on company business, are legal and roadworthy and that every driver is trained and medically fit.

The Competition Act is gaining momentum in its scope and impact. In essence the Competition Act attacks anti-competitive agreements and abuses of a dominant position. Anyone who breaches the Act can at present be fined up to 10% of their gross UK turnover. This includes small companies who fix prices across a local market as well as the well publicised larger companies with dominant market positions. Around 500 cases are investigated by the Office of Fair Trading every year. Directors are counselled to be very careful about discussing prices with competitors.

The list of legislation impacting upon an organisation is endless - The Data Protection Act, Health and Safety Act, Environmental Protection Act, various European Community directives etc. It is important that directors keep abreast with changes in the law and are able to understand their impact as part of a risk assessment. It will be prudent for companies to insure against civil actions that may be taken against their directors and officers; this is known as D&O insurance. Even a small claim can be ruinous for a director if it has to be borne personally by him or her.

Board legal risk assessment

	Low	High
High	Contingency H&S, EPA, Director Disqualification, Insolvency Act	Primary Litigation by employees and customers
Low	House-keeping Fraud Data Protection Act	Monitoring & Review Companies Act Industry Regulation

Impact (vertical axis) — **Likelihood** (horizontal axis)

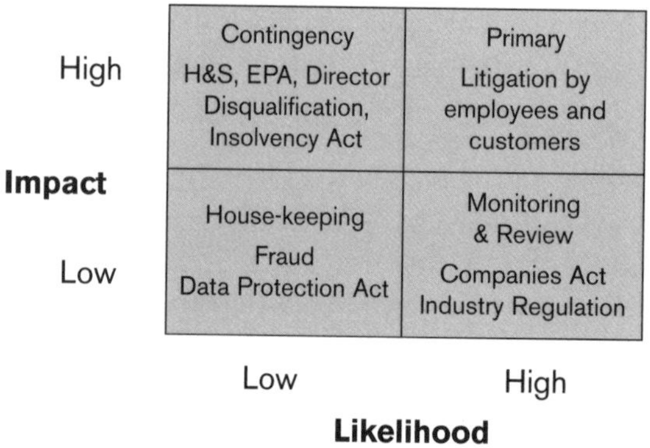

figure 11.1 Board legal risk assessment

The Combined Code

The Combined Code is an evolving code of conduct which applies to listed companies. Boards are expected to 'comply or explain' when deviating from the Code but there are no legal penalties for non-conformance. Derek Higgs, in his letter to the Chancellor of the 20thJanuary 2003 (**Higgs**) captured the innate benefits of codes over legislation; "The brittleness and rigidity of legislation cannot dictate the behaviour, or foster the trust, I believe is fundamental to the effective unitary board and to superior corporate performance."

In his recommendations to further change the Combined Code he stated "Corporate failure, of course, will always be with us. Enterprise creates prosperity but involves risk. No system of governance can or should fully protect companies and investors from their own mistakes. We can, however, reasonably hope that boardroom sins of commission or omission - whether strategy, performance or oversight - are minimised."

Conclusion

This chapter is a sad reflection upon the relationship between the director, the limited company and the law. What is supposed to be a shield of trust between the company, its directors and society has instead become the sword of Government aimed at directors as they struggle to ensure conformity and further undermines the assumption of faith and trust that lies at the heart of the fiduciary duty of directors. The general uncertainty about the meaning of the new laws is a massive problem for directors. It was Hayek who provided the standard on the rule of law: "Government in all its actions is bound by rules fixed and announced beforehand - rules which make it possible to foresee with fair certainty how the authority will use its coercive powers in given circumstances and to plan one's individual affairs on the basis of this knowledge." (**Hayek, F.**) This is plainly not the case currently for the beleaguered director.

In particular, directors should be wary of trading whilst insolvent. A properly trained and renewed director should be fully conversant with their company's financial statements and able to take remedial action.

As a general rule, companies should operate within the law of their host country, but the rigid application of legislation can have serious cost consequences for organisations as well as unintended consequences. Directors can make their views known through lobbying organisations such as the IOD, CBI or the various Trade Associations. These organisations can also be useful sources of low-cost advice on conformance to the law as well as representing companies in legal disputes and often legal fees for advice are 'wrapped up' within membership fees.

Conformance to evolving codes of conduct is increasingly seen by regulators as the way forward but the expansion of legislation and regulation is a dangerous trend that risks squeezing the lifeblood out of an organisation.

CHAPTER 12 - LOOKING TO THE FUTURE

Through its long history, the limited company has taken many different forms and been used for many different purposes. It has been found to be highly adaptable and there is no doubt that it will continue to be so in the future. The duty of faithfulness that lay at the centre of its original purpose continues to provide opportunities for reflection and renewal as the director of today works under the spotlight of accountability that is a feature of our times. Directors will be watched increasingly closely as investors, shareholders and other stakeholders observe ways in which faithfulness can be eroded and comment upon the obligation directors have for faithful service that the role has always implied.

The model of the director as a 'good steward' which has been developed in this book can help them find new ways to act faithfully in the future. Nothing less than excellence will be expected!

One thing is for certain: There will be no let-up in the public focus upon the role of the director in corporate governance and, if anything, the pace will increase. Amongst the most recent issues raised have been:

- The focus upon minority rights and diversity in the workplace to which boards of directors must respond: New rules which require companies to provide staff with quiet places for reflection and prayer at work and flexible working arrangements for staff who are parents or carers who may need additional holiday entitlements. **(Commission for Racial Equality)**

- The tendency for central government to interfere with the work of boards of directors: The DTI intend to introduce a requirement for companies to produce each year a 'Operating & Financial Review (OFR) which should describe information about the company's policy towards its staff, customers and suppliers as well as its wider impact upon the environment, social impact and the wider community. **(The Times)**

- The effect that the 'goldfish bowl' is having upon the recruitment of badly needed fresh talent to Boardroom UK: The endless speculation about what goes on in the boardroom and the increasingly onerous reporting requirements about the pay and contracts of directors **(Sunday Times)**

- The tendency for boards of directors to reward failure: The chairman of Network Rail has demanded that his senior executives should be paid bonuses of up to £270,000 each out of public funds although the company has failed to meet its targets for train punctuality. **(Sunday Telegraph)**

These are only a few examples of the way that discussion about directors and their roles and responsibilities continues to excite the interest of not only the media but also wider society. In addition, there are some deeper issues to address that may affect the future of the role of the director and the way that he or she will discharge their duty of faithfulness.

Overview

Whatever is predicted will be different from what occurs, of that we may be sure! But there are a number of trends that are generally accepted. For example, that there will be no slowing down in the opening up of markets which will continue to be highly competitive but that whilst there will be ample access to finance, technology and markets should a company need them, it is people who will remain highly unpredictable. There will be fewer people available as the demographics move against working aged individuals; education and training standards will not show a marked improvement and contrary views about the worth of the company, its place in society and the role of its directors will continue to be debated.

For example, trends may include:

- Consumers resist the concentration of power in a few national and global brands and use the Internet to spread 'bad news' and mischievous stories about supposed company malpractice. This means greater pressure will be placed upon directors to provide clear standards and transparent reporting.

- Prospective employees select their employer of choice rather than the other way around. This means that the virtues of the company will be scrutinised before any commitment is made and that induction, training and career development will be critical as a way to retain and build loyalty alongside the example of leadership that the company's directors provide.

- Investors, shareholders and stakeholders all demand more information and access to the board's decision making processes. This means that boards of directors will need to be clear about from where their power and authority comes and the way they are going to demonstrate that they have been good stewards of the company's assets and activities.

- Individuals appreciate the complexities of the role of director and demand information and knowledge before they are willing to consider an appointment as a director. This means that companies will need to provide personal and professional development resources and support both before and throughout the duration of the appointment.

- *'People will only trust those they trust to understand them'* and will make more demands upon companies not only that they should appreciate individual aspirations but also that they should implement policies and practices in the workplace that are sensitive to cultural diversity and to its varied meanings.

All of this adds up to a future agenda that will include the compliance and conformity demanded of companies and their directors by society, the intense pressures arising from local and global competition and the nature of employees with complex aspirations whilst ensuring high performance. All these factors and more will test directors and their role of corporate governors to the full.

The globalisation of governance

Corporate governance has become a global issue. This in not only about the ease of communications across the world so that information is universally available but also because we are all shareholders now: Almost all of us have stakes in companies throughout the world as part of our pension arrangements. The crash in US markets which was triggered by the Enron scandal and the collapse of Arthur Anderson, caused problems not only in US but across the world and from which stocks have still not recovered. The Parmalat crash came closer to home and the affairs of Equitable Life, Marconi and the continuing destruction of the value in the shares of Marks and Spencer have all concentrated the minds of regulators.

Good corporate governance in the future will not be an option, it will be mandatory - but not regulated - and whilst it may appear at present to be a topic that effects larger and publicly quoted companies only, the standards developed for this sector will inevitably be felt in the small and medium sized private company sector also. In April 2004 the OECD in Paris issued its first global guidance for corporate governance building upon the UK's experience of codes of conduct which are considered to be in advance of the practice in most other countries and more reliant upon encouraging good governance than the USA's Sarbanes Oxley Act which is all compliance and penalty. All compliance and penalty will place at risk the development of enterprising and innovating activity which is a key ingredient of successful companies.

In countries where companies are encouraged to develop their own standards in corporate governance higher levels of inward investment will be attracted whilst countries with governments that impose standards through regulation will help to create hidden barriers against inward investment. A healthy climate for corporate governance will be one in which trust and good faith are the norm.

Governance as competitive advantage

If people are going to be the key determinant factor for success in the future, inspiring and leading people will be a prime role for the board and directors. This means that an increasing amount of time will be spent by the board discussing issues about employees. One way this can be initiated will be, at the very least, to re-visit the principles that lie behind the Investors in People Award and to ensure that the basics of manpower planning, recruitment, selection and induction of employees are all in place. Thereafter, directors will need to encourage high performance by conducting regular surveys of employee satisfaction which will take questioning beyond feel good and housekeeping factors and into areas about the way that the board uses its power and authority and how these are felt in the organisation. This will include 360 degree reviews but will go well beyond them. Unless the board and its directors are trusted, its leadership will only be grudgingly acknowledged and the company's performance will remain ordinary. When the board acts to indicate its own performance in this way it is showing not only its confidence in its own virtues but also it is being faithful to the charge given to it by its owners and shareholders. This is the real test of the good steward!

Training for the board

If there was ever a time for the gifted amateur at the board, it is no longer an option now! 'Buggins turn', 'I play golf with him' and 'my family have known them for ever' have never been good reasons for making board appointments, but making the right appointments have never been so vital. The appointment of individuals who have the knowledge needed to direct the company as it moves forward into the future should be one of the most important tasks for the board. Although the initial stages of the board recruitment process is often delegated to the chairman or a small committee of the board, it should be a matter in which the whole board is involved as it will be one of the single most important acts that the board will complete. Candidates will need not only knowledge in company direction but also experience of people and their motivations together with the confidence to participate in lively debate in the boardroom.

It will be the reflective practitioner and learner director who has the potential to make the most contribution to the board through the appreciation that he or she has of not only the company's markets and competitive environment but also of contemporary culture and of meaning making. This knowledge needs to be acquired and cultural sensitivity needs to be tested. This is the reason that the idea of governance as education is appealing: It does not assume that because an individual has attained the rank or title of director that he or she no longer has anything more to learn. On the contrary, it assumes that because the individual aspires to become a good steward that he or she understands that they have much to learn.

The concept of a School of Governance referred to in Chapter 9 is designed to alert present and future directors to the benefits of learning with the aim of becoming a professional director. The appointment of a director to the board based upon experience alone can be downright dangerous; directing is quite a different activity to managing. This will never be a sufficient substitute for learning and amongst the qualities of an individual who aspires to become a professional director will be:

- The ability to identify their own learning needs and find ways to fulfill them

- Independence of mind, confident and willing to express unpopular views, when needed

- Knowledgeable about the Companies Act and the various Codes of Conduct that apply to work of directors

- Sensitive to changes taking place in contemporary culture and the ability to interpret their significance for the company in discussion with colleagues

The Government plans to introduce the first draft of a new Companies Act for debate as a Green Paper in Parliament (Appendix 4.). This makes specific reference to directors being required to have the knowledge and skills to take the right decisions for the company as good stewards. In the event of a challenge, they could be tested about their understanding of their roles and responsibilities as directors and disqualified if found wanting. This test of the performance of directors goes well beyond the existing requirements.

Standards at the board

It would be too simple to say that what the public sees of the behaviour of boards reflects low standards, but the 'rewarding failure' debate has raised eyebrows about what kind of world some directors inhabit. This implies that directors can become disconnected with other people's feelings and end up disregarding their duty of faithfulness and 'right relationship' with their shareholders or the standards of the wider society in which the company is set. There is something repugnant about the responses that 'fat cats' make when they are challenged and the justification they make for large amounts of incentive payments or share options. Recent examples are leading inevitably to demands for new ways to control all directors because of the greed of a very few. Any such regulations can only prejudice the rights of directors who are good stewards and who appreciate their responsibilities for 'right relationship' with others. Examples of the increasing concern of investor groups have been shown at AGMs when they have called for restraint and questioned board decisions about rewards.

The standards that the board sets for the discharge of the duties of its directors and the board as a whole will form the basis for its corporate governance activities. Much of this can be taken from the various codes of conduct available and adapted but each board will reflect upon its own particular circumstances and build upon the basic standards shown. In particular, each board will wish to develop absolute clarity about where power and authority lies and the areas of the company's policy and practice which the board reserves to itself. These standards should be published in written form as guidance for the members of the board.

Setting standards at the board is a vital task and should go beyond pious statements of intent such as are beginning to appear in the Annual Reports of some larger companies: 'We will respect the environment' or 'we value our staff'. Such statements can only be made meaningful if they are tested regularly and if continual improvements are achieved. *People will only trust those they trust to understand them.*

There will be an increase in the use of qualitative indicators of the performance of directors alongside the more usual quantitative indicators of increases in profits and share price to determine executive pay and reward. Such qualitative standards will include issues such as power, authority and leadership:

- How has the company's collective leadership style impacted upon performance and results: Do people feel able to exercise their creativity or are they fearful of being found out?

- How has the board's promotion of its aim been communicated: Are employees confident and clear about what is expected of them or is there a 'Not me Guv' attitude?

- Is the board honest about its own working methods and relationships: Does each director feel able to dissent from the strongly held views of others without fear and be listened to with respect?

- Is the board clear about who its key stakeholders are: Does the board meet with its stakeholders regularly and seek their opinions - even the most difficult?

Suits v ear-rings!

Diversity can be a word that smacks of political correctness for its own sake but whilst the UK is one of the most 'open' economies in the world in terms of volume of trade, only c.7% of non-executive directors in the UK are not of British origin. This is a serious shortcoming when an understanding of global markets, culture and consumers is a key skill needed in the boardroom for the effective development of business strategies that will add value to sales. Similarly, only c.4% of executive director posts and 6 % of non-executive director posts are held by women.

In addition, although over two thirds of UK companies are less than 10 years old, the overall impression is Corporate UK Ltd. is run by 55+ year old white male 'suits'.

Whilst this generalization may be an exaggeration, too many companies lack real flair, innovation and courage when it comes to making appointments to the board. The idea that the board should have one 'ear-ring' wearing member highlights the need for individuals from different backgrounds from the usual corporate mould and for diversity in the approach and thinking needed at board level. For example, in the USA a number of web sites sign post the 'Top Ten Companies for Latinos' as a way to attract the best employees and as global markets develop the 'personality' of boards will be a 'shop window' for stakeholders and interested consumers. Boards need to start developing pools of diverse talent from which they can draw that will improve the balance, debate, dissent and decision-making on the board.

Good stewardship v regulation

At present there is a drive into regulation at the expense of good stewardship. This drive is about the apparent lack of trust that other people and institutions outside of the company have about the way a board of directors may be tempted to behave - that is selfishly and as agents with too little regard for their duty of faithfulness and too much regard for their own interests - and therefore the need for protecting themselves through, the creation at best, of codes of conduct and, at worst, of more legislation. This potential removal of the director's own motivation which is to do their best by their appointment to fulfill their duty of faithfulness -which applies to 99% of all directors - is the most serious threat that directors will face in the future. These pressures will include:

- More information available to investors, employees and the public about companies and their progress and more 'transparency' through the free distribution of data via the Internet and 'rogue' web sites

- Greater diversity throughout the workforce and the implementation of policies by central and local government designed to increase social inclusion and access to work

- A focus upon the individual rights of employees with opportunities for career development through flexible working practices and upon consumers rights for fair dealing from companies

- A desire by central government to protect shareholders, other stakeholders and the public from corporate wrongdoing which can lead to financial loss when the potential risks of investment have not been made clear in advance which is a particular issue in the financial services sectors

Therefore the recent drive towards codes reinforced by regulation and legislation needs to be replaced - or at least greatly moderated by directors demonstrating clearly their commitment to good governance and this will be more than the appointment of governance Czars in the boardroom, the setting up of a raft of board sub-committees or statements of achievement in Annual Reports. What will be needed is a fundamental change in the way that directors think, feel and act with regards their duty of faithfulness: They will need to be renewed. Some will fail to appreciate the scale of the changes needed, be resistant and have to be removed; others will rise to the challenge; all will learn from the experience. No codes, regulation or legislation, should be allowed to diminish the rights of directors to be responsible as good stewards - that is, their duty of faithfulness - which so many directors have learned and earned in the past and which future generations of directors will do in the future.

Shareholders v stakeholders

Directors are appointed to do their best for the company as its agents. The first duty of the director is to make a profit and to create a sustainable and successful future for it. It will be a matter of common sense that directors will take into account when taking their decisions that it will develop positive relationships with those with whom it needs to be in 'right relationship' in order to reach its desired future. This can include other stakeholders that go beyond its own investor-shareholders including suppliers, employees and the community in which it is set. All companies are local companies, even when they operate globally. The board will therefore reflect upon its stakeholders and agree ways in which their perspectives can be aligned with the company's aim or the company's practices changed.

The first draft of a new Companies Act, referred to already, makes specific reference to directors taking the interests of stakeholders into account in their decision making and this too may be tested.

Transparency v Secrecy

Secrecy is the enemy of trust. Secrecy destroys trust. Secrecy speaks of patronage and exclusivity. Of course, it is understood that there are secrets in organisations, these are called the intellectual property rights or IPR of the company and in the Knowledge Age can often be a major part of the value of the company's assets. We are not talking about these secrets which are commercially confidential and which should not be shared with competitors or stolen by employees.

What we are speaking of is the way that some directors have used such confidentiality to avoid answering awkward questions that it is their duty to do. One example recently has been the publication of email correspondence by senior executives at Shell: There was a deliberate practice of the non-disclosure of damaging information that could have affected the value of its shares on the market over a long period of time. Such secrecy is contrary to the role of the good steward and has risked destroying the reputation of Shell.

Transparency is hard. Transparency means owning up to mistakes and failure. Transparency speaks of the recovery of 'right relationship' with others and of starting over again. In an age when the both the speed and ease of communication and access to new technology has transformed business practice, transparency will be the norm. Not only will the activities of directors be subject to more scrutiny but directors will also be expected to explain more. Annual Reports will therefore be less about what the company did and more about the reasons that lay behind its actions. Directors will become more accountable. This means that the board's discussions about its future strategy and the clarity with which it is able to communicate this to its investor-shareholders and other stakeholders will become even more important; People will only trust those they trust to understand them. The question that directors will ask themselves will not be; 'What should we tell others' but: 'Is there anything here that we should not tell others?' Amongst the questions that directors will ask themselves about their communications will be:

- Do we have a communications strategy that is based upon transparency?

- Do we publish everything we are able about the company that will be helpful to our investor-shareholders and our other stakeholders?

- Do we ensure that we use plain English in all our communications and test other people's ability to understand them?

- If we make a mistake, do we ensure that any misunderstandings are corrected as soon as possible?

- Do we invite our employees and our other stakeholders to question and answer sessions?

The next steps

It is the role of the board to take the company into an uncertain future and to deal with high levels of unpredictability. No one else has this responsibility - it resides with each individual director and the board. What actions can the board take to shape the future? Shown below is a task that will help individual directors and boards to decide where their time should be focused compared to where they are actually spending their time and resources at present. Score 'Current board focus' on a scale 1-7 and then score the way the board's energies should be directed. This will show the gaps that require further work to ensure that the board will work more effectively in the future.

Task	Current board focus	Future board focus	Gap analysis
Strategic direction	1 2 3 4 5 6 7	1 2 3 4 5 6 7	
Policy development	1 2 3 4 5 6 7	1 2 3 4 5 6 7	
Supervising executive	1 2 3 4 5 6 7	1 2 3 4 5 6 7	
CEO appraisal	1 2 3 4 5 6 7	1 2 3 4 5 6 7	
Board information flows	1 2 3 4 5 6 7	1 2 3 4 5 6 7	
Risk management	1 2 3 4 5 6 7	1 2 3 4 5 6 7	
Accountability to stakeholders	1 2 3 4 5 6 7	1 2 3 4 5 6 7	
Corporate governance	1 2 3 4 5 6 7	1 2 3 4 5 6 7	
Building trust	1 2 3 4 5 6 7	1 2 3 4 5 6 7	
Director duties	1 2 3 4 5 6 7	1 2 3 4 5 6 7	
Board behaviours	1 2 3 4 5 6 7	1 2 3 4 5 6 7	

Conclusion

Being a director is an honourable profession and vocation which needs to be learned. This is not only about the skills needed for the job as it is now but also the willingness and the ability to change and adapt as the way that the limited company is viewed by society alters and new meanings for it are developed. Directors are always the 'good stewards' of what is usually other people's property; they are trusted and they are faithful to the objects of the company. Good stewardship requires application and understanding and it needs to be experienced and reflected upon continually. Individual directors - and the board of which they are members - have the responsibility for the future prosperity of the company, for its relationships with others and, through its activity, the opportunity to contribute to the health of society as a whole. This is a role that is worth renewing!

Eight ways to renew the role of the director

1   The role is vocational and a 'calling' that demands faithful service

2   Respect and trust come from meeting the highest standards of personal and professional conduct

3   The role of the director is to lead. This means developing a personal leadership style and leading the company purposely into the future

4   The director is the steward of the assets of others; this requires continuous attention to accountability

5   Every director of the company and member of the board is equally responsible for good corporate governance

6   Directors should govern, management should manage

7   Foster and practice a culture of open dissent and value debate at the board to break the bonds of inertia

8   Trust is a personal choice and is within our own sphere of responsibility - exercise it!

APPENDICES

APPENDIX 1 - FIGURES & TABLES

APPENDIX 2 - REFERENCES

Chapter One

Bastiat's, 'The Law', reprinted 1998, IEA, London

Reagan, R. Reagan Library, California

Neil Collins, Daily Telegraph 08/09/2003

Fred Goodwin, quoted in The Herald, 20th Feb, 2003

Denning, L., in HL Bolton (Engineering) Co Ltd v TJ Graham & Sons Ltd

Luke, Chapter 8: verse17

OECD, 'Principles on Corporate Governance', Paris, April 1999

Maw et al., 'What is Corporate Governance', 1994

J. Wolfensohn, quoted by an article in the *Financial Times*, June 21, 1999.

Tricker, R., 'International Corporate Governance, Prentice Hall , London, 1994

Sir Adrian Cadbury, 'The Director's Manual', Director Books, Simon & Schuster, 1990

Chapter Two

Micklethwait, J. & Wooldridge A., 'The Company - A Short History of a Revolutionary Idea', Weidenfeld & Nicolson, London, 2003

Collins and Porrus, 'Building Your Company's Vision', Harvard Business Review, Sept/Oct 1996

John Paul II, 'Laborem Exercens, Rome, 1981

Chapter Three

IOD, 'Guidelines for Directors, London, 1985

Drucker P., quoted in Mickethwait & Wooldridge

Ibid, Micklethwait and Wooldridge

Blackstone, quoted in IOD, 'Role of the Director' course notes, London, 2001

Strategy Unit, Cabinet Office 'Private Action, Public Benefit:A Review of the Charities & the Wider Not-For-Profit Sector, 2001

Chapter Four

MORI Surveys, 1999-2004

The Committee on Standards in Public Life, 1996

Chapter Five

Slessor, T., 'Ministries of Deception', Aurum Press, London, 2002

Hughes G., 'Open Government - What do we need to know?', Ed. Platten, S, Canterbury Press, Norwich, 2003

Hollenbach, D. 'The Common Good & Christian Ethics', Cambridge University Press, Cambridge, 2002

O'Neill, O., 'A Question of Trust', Cambridge University Press, Cambridge, 2002

Fowler, J.W., 'Stages of Faith', HarperCollins, New York, 1981

Chapter Six

Mathew, chapter 25, verses 14-30

Block, P., 'Stewardship - Choosing Service Over Self Interest' Berrett-Koehler Publishers, SanFrancisco,1993

Harvey Jones, J., quoted in 'Role of the Company Director & the Board', IOD, London, 2001

Renton, T., 'Standards for the Board', IOD, Kogan Page, London, 2001

De Bono, E., 'Opportunities: A Handbook of Business Opportunity Search', Penguin, London, 1980

Zohar, D., 'Rewiring the Corporate Brain', Berrett-Koehler, San Francisco, 1997

Mintoff, J. & Denton E.,'A Spiritual Audit of Corporate America'; Jossey-Bass Inc; San Francisco, 1999

Sternberg. E., 'Just Business, Business Ethics in Action', Little, Brown and co, London, 1994

Sternberg, E., 'Corporate Governance: Accountability in the Marketplace', IEA, London, 2004

Cardinal Renato Martino, International Conference of Christian Business Executives, Rome, March 2004

Chapter Seven

Hoose, B.,'Authority in the Roman Catholic Church', Lash, N. Ed., Ashgate, Aldershot, 2002

Chapter Eight

Senge, P.,'The Fifth Discipline', Random House, London, 1990

Adair, J.,'The Leadership of Jesus',Canterbury Press, Norwich, 2001

Ibid. Zohar, D.

Fowler, J.W.,'Faithful Change' Abingdon Press, Nashville, 1996

Chapter Nine

Ibid., Hoose, B.

Schon, D.,'The Reflective Practitioner', Ashgate/Arena, 1991

Garratt, B.,'The Learning Organisation', Gower, Aldershot, 1987

Schwartz, P., 'When Good Companies do bad things', John Wiley, New York, 1999

Chapter Ten

Higgs, 'Review of the Role and Effectiveness of Non-Executive Directors', 2003

Sonnenfeld, J., 'What Makes Boards Great', HBR, Sept. 2002

Tricker, B., 'Role of Company Director course notes', IOD, London, 1998

The Turnbull Report, 'Internal Control: Guidance for Directors on the Combined Code', 1999

Chapter Eleven

DTI, quoted on www.dti.gov.uk

Myerson, J.,The Daily Telegraph, 10th June 2004

DTI., 'Routes to Resolution: Improving Dispute resolution in Britain', July 2001

Anderson, S., Small Business Council Research reported in The Daily Telegraph, 8th March, 2004

IOD and CMS Cameron McKenna, 'Under Pressure - Are Britain's directors feeling the heat? 2003

Ibid., Higgs

Hayek, F.A., 'The Road to Serfdom', Routledge, London, 1944

Chapter Twelve

Commission for Racial Equality reported in the Sunday Telegraph 2nd May, 2004

The Times 5th May, 2004

Sunday Times 9th May, 2004

Sunday Telegraph 16th May, 2004

APPENDIX 3 - USEFUL WEB SITES

Faith in Governance www.faithingovernance.com

AGENDA; Social Responsibility in Scotland	www.agenda-scotland.org
Charity Commission for England & Wales	www.charity-commission.gov.uk
Companies House	www.companieshouse.gov.uk
Corporate Governance Website	www.corpgov.net
DTI	www.dti.gov.uk
ECGI International Codes & Principles	www.ecgi.org
European Corporate Governance Service	www.ecgs.net
Financial Reporting Council	www.frc.org.uk
Global Corporate Governance Forum	www.gcgf.org
Institute of Chartered Accountants - England & Wales	www.icaew.co.uk
The Corporate Governance Unit	www.scottishdirector.com
The Corporate Library	www.thecorporatelibrary.com
The Institute of Directors	www.iod.com
The International Institute for Corporate Governance	www.iicg.som.yale.edu/
The Office of the Scottish Charity Regulator	www.oscr.org.uk
US Security and Exchanges Commission	www.sec.gov

APPENDIX 4 - THE COMBINED CODE ON CORPORATE GOVERNANCE

CODE OF BEST PRACTICE
Section 1 Companies

A. DIRECTORS

A.1 The Board

Main Principle

Every company should be headed by an effective board, which is collectively responsible for the success of the company.

Supporting Principles

The board's role is to provide entrepreneurial leadership of the company within a framework of prudent and effective controls which enables risk to be assessed and managed. The board should set the company's strategic aims, ensure that the necessary financial and human resources are in place for the company to meet its objectives and review management performance. The board should set the company's values and standards and ensure that its obligations to its shareholders and others are understood and met. All directors must take decisions objectively in the interests of the company. As part of their role as members of a unitary board, non-executive directors should constructively challenge and help develop proposals on strategy. Non-executive directors should scrutinise the performance of management in meeting agreed goals and objectives and monitor the reporting of performance. They should satisfy themselves on the integrity of financial information and that financial controls and systems of risk management are robust and defensible. They are responsible for determining appropriate levels of remuneration of executive directors and have a prime role in appointing, and where necessary removing, executive directors, and in succession planning.

Code Provisions

A.1.1 The board should meet sufficiently regularly to discharge its duties effectively. There should be a formal schedule of matters specifically reserved for its decision. The annual report should include a statement of how the board operates, including a high level statement of which types of decisions are to be taken by the board and which are to be delegated to management.

A.1.2 The annual report should identify the chairman, the deputy chairman (where there is one), the chief executive, the senior independent director and the chairmen and members of the nomination, audit and remuneration committees. It should also set out the number of meetings of the board and those committees and individual attendance by directors.

A.1.3 The chairman should hold meetings with the non-executive directors without the executives present. Led by the senior independent director, the non-executive directors should meet without the chairman present at least annually to appraise the chairman's performance (as described in A.6.1) and on such other occasions as are deemed appropriate.

A.1.4 Where directors have concerns which cannot be resolved about the running of the company or a proposed action, they should ensure that their concerns are recorded in the board minutes. On resignation, a non-executive director should provide a written statement to the chairman, for circulation to the board, if they have any such concerns.

A.1.5 The company should arrange appropriate insurance cover in respect of legal action against its directors.

A.2 Chairman and chief executive

Main Principle

There should be a clear division of responsibilities at the head of the company between the running of the board and the executive responsibility for the running of the company's business. No one individual should have unfettered powers of decision.

Supporting Principle

The chairman is responsible for leadership of the board, ensuring its effectiveness on all aspects of its role and setting its agenda. The chairman is also responsible for ensuring that the directors receive accurate, timely and clear information. The chairman should ensure effective communication with shareholders. The chairman should also facilitate the effective contribution of non-executive directors in particular and ensure constructive relations between executive and non-executive directors.

Code Provisions

A.2.1 The roles of chairman and chief executive should not be exercised by the same individual. The division of responsibilities between the chairman and chief executive should be clearly established, set out in writing and agreed by the board.

A.2.2 The chairman should on appointment meet the independence criteria set out in A.3.1 below. A chief executive should not go on to be chairman of the same company. If exceptionally a board decides that a chief executive should become chairman, the board should consult major shareholders in advance and should set out its reasons to shareholders at the time of the appointment and in the next annual report.

A.3 Board balance and independence

Main Principle

The board should include a balance of executive and non-executive directors (and in particular independent non-executive directors) such that no individual or small group of individuals can dominate the board's decision taking.

Supporting Principles

The board should not be so large as to be unwieldy. The board should be of sufficient size that the balance of skills and experience is appropriate for the requirements of the business and that changes to the board's composition can be managed without undue disruption. To ensure that power and information are not concentrated in one or two individuals, there should be a strong presence on the board of both executive and non-executive directors. The value of ensuring that committee membership is refreshed and that undue reliance is not placed on particular individuals should be taken into account in deciding chairmanship and membership of committees. No one other than the committee chairman and members is entitled to be present at a meeting of the nomination, audit or remuneration committee, but others may attend at the invitation of the committee.

Code provisions

A.3.1 The board should identify in the annual report each non-executive director it considers to be independent. The board should determine whether the director is independent in character and judgement and whether there are relationships or circumstances which are likely to affect, or could appear to affect, the director's judgement.

The board should state its reasons if it determines that a director is independent notwithstanding the existence of relationships or circumstances which may appear relevant to its determination, including if the director: has been an employee of the company or group within the last five years; has, or has had within the last three years, a material business relationship with the company either directly, or as a partner, shareholder, director or senior employee of a body that has such a relationship with the company; has received or receives additional remuneration from the company apart from a director's fee, participates in the company's share option or a performance-related pay scheme, or is a member of the company's pension scheme; has close family ties with any of the company's advisers, directors or senior employees; holds cross-directorships or has significant links with other directors through involvement in other companies or bodies; represents a significant shareholder; or has served on the board for more than nine years from the date of their first election.

A.3.2 Except for smaller companies, at least half the board, excluding the chairman, should comprise non-executive directors determined by the board to be independent. A smaller company should have at least two independent non-executive directors.

A.3.3 The board should appoint one of the independent non-executive directors to be the senior independent director. The senior independent director should be available to shareholders if they have concerns which contact through the normal channels of chairman, chief executive or finance director has failed to resolve or for which such contact is inappropriate.

A.4 Appointments to the Board

Main Principle

There should be a formal, rigorous and transparent procedure for the appointment of new directors to the board.

Supporting Principles

Appointments to the board should be made on merit and against objective criteria. Care should be taken to ensure that appointees have enough time available to devote to the job. This is particularly important in the case of chairmanships. The board should satisfy itself that plans are in place for orderly succession for appointments to the board and to senior management, so as to maintain an appropriate balance of skills and experience within the company and on the board.

Code Provisions

A.4.1 There should be a nomination committee which should lead the process for board appointments and make recommendations to the board. A majority of members of the nomination committee should be independent non-executive directors. The chairman or an independent non-executive director should chair the committee, but the chairman should not chair the nomination committee when it is dealing with the appointment of a successor to the chairmanship. The nomination committee should make available its terms of reference, explaining its role and the authority delegated to it by the board.

A.4.2 The nomination committee should evaluate the balance of skills, knowledge and experience on the board and, in the light of this evaluation, prepare a description of the role and capabilities required for a particular appointment.

A.4.3 For the appointment of a chairman, the nomination committee should prepare a job specification, including an assessment of the time commitment expected, recognising the need for availability in the event of crises. A chairman's other significant commitments should be disclosed to the board before appointment and included in the annual report. Changes to such commitments should be reported to the board as they arise, and included in the next annual report. No individual should be appointed to a second chairmanship of a FTSE 100 company.

A.4.4 The terms and conditions of appointment of non-executive directors should be made available for inspection. The letter of appointment should set out the expected time commitment. Non-executive directors should undertake that they will have sufficient time to meet what is expected of them. Their other significant commitments should be disclosed to the board before appointment, with a broad indication of the time involved and the board should be informed of subsequent changes.

A.4.5 The board should not agree to a full time executive director taking on more than one non-executive directorship in a FTSE 100 company nor the chairmanship of such a company.

A.4.6 A separate section of the annual report should describe the work of the nomination committee, including the process it has used in relation to board appointments. An explanation should be given if neither an external search consultancy nor open advertising has been used in the appointment of a chairman or a non-executive director.

A.5 Information and professional development

Main Principle

The board should be supplied in a timely manner with information in a form and of a quality appropriate to enable it to discharge its duties. All directors should receive induction on joining the board and should regularly update and refresh their skills and knowledge.

Supporting Principles

The chairman is responsible for ensuring that the directors receive accurate, timely and clear information. Management has an obligation to provide such information but directors should seek clarification or amplification where necessary. The chairman should ensure that the directors continually update their skills and the knowledge and familiarity with the company required to fulfil their role both on the board and on board committees. The company should provide the necessary resources for eveloping and updating its directors' knowledge and capabilities. Under the direction of the chairman, the company secretary's responsibilities include ensuring good information flows within the board and its committees and between senior management and non-executive directors, as well as facilitating induction and assisting with professional development as required. The company secretary should be responsible for advising the board through the chairman on all governance matters.

Code Provisions

A.5.1 The chairman should ensure that new directors receive a full, formal and tailored induction on joining the board. As part of this, the company should offer to major shareholders the opportunity to meet a new non-executive director.

A.5.2 The board should ensure that directors, especially non-executive directors, have access to independent professional advice at the company's expense where they judge it necessary to discharge their responsibilities as directors. Committees should be provided with sufficient resources to undertake their duties.

A.5.3 All directors should have access to the advice and services of the company secretary, who is responsible to the board for ensuring that board procedures are complied with. Both the appointment and removal of the company secretary should be a matter for the board as a whole.

A.6 Performance evaluation

Main Principle

The board should undertake a formal and rigorous annual evaluation of its own performance and that of its committees and individual directors.

Supporting Principle

Individual evaluation should aim to show whether each director continues to contribute effectively and to demonstrate commitment to the role (including commitment of time for board and committee meetings and any other duties). The chairman should act on the results of the performance evaluation by recognising the strengths and addressing the weaknesses of the board and, where appropriate, proposing new members be appointed to the board or seeking the resignation of directors.

Code Provision

A.6.1 The board should state in the annual report how performance evaluation of the board, its committees and its individual directors has been conducted. The non-executive directors, led by the senior independent director, should be responsible for performance evaluation of the chairman, taking into account the views of executive directors.

A.7 Re-election

Main Principle

All directors should be submitted for re-election at regular intervals, subject to continued satisfactory performance. The board should ensure planned and progressive refreshing of the board.

Code Provisions

A.7.1 All directors should be subject to election by shareholders at the first annual general meeting after their appointment, and to re-election thereafter at intervals of no more than three years. The names of directors submitted for election or re-election should be accompanied by sufficient biographical details and any other relevant information to enable shareholders to take an informed decision on their election.

A.7.2 Non-executive directors should be appointed for specified terms subject to re-election and to Companies Acts provisions relating to the removal of a director. The board should set out to shareholders in the papers accompanying a resolution to elect a non-executive director why they believe an individual should be elected. The chairman should confirm to shareholders when proposing re-election that, following formal performance evaluation, the individual's performance continues to be effective and to demonstrate commitment to the role. Any term beyond six years (e.g. two three-year terms) for a non-executive director should be subject to particularly rigorous review, and should take into account the need for progressive refreshing of the board. Non-executive directors may serve longer than nine years (e.g. three three-year terms), subject to annual re-election. Serving more than nine years could be relevant to the determination of a non-executive director's independence (as set out in provision A.3.1).

B.   REMUNERATION

B.1   The Level and Make-up of Remuneration

Main Principles

Levels of remuneration should be sufficient to attract, retain and motivate directors of the quality required to run the company successfully, but a company should avoid paying more than is necessary for this purpose. A significant proportion of executive directors' remuneration should be structured so as to link rewards to corporate and individual performance.

Supporting Principle

The remuneration committee should judge where to position their company relative to other companies. But they should use such comparisons with caution, in view of the risk of an upward ratchet of remuneration levels with no corresponding improvement in performance. They should also be sensitive to pay and employment conditions elsewhere in the group, especially when determining annual salary increases.

Code Provisions

Remuneration policy

B.1.1 The performance-related elements of remuneration should form a significant proportion of the total remuneration package of executive directors and should be designed to align their interests with those of shareholders and to give these directors keen incentives to perform at the highest levels. In designing schemes of performance-related remuneration, the remuneration committee should follow the provisions in Schedule A to this Code.

B.1.2 Executive share options should not be offered at a discount save as permitted by the relevant provisions of the Listing Rules.

B.1.3 Levels of remuneration for non-executive directors should reflect the time commitment and responsibilities of the role. Remuneration for nonexecutive directors should not include share options. If, exceptionally, options are granted, shareholder approval should be sought in advance and any shares acquired by exercise of the options should be held until at least one year after the non-executive director leaves the board. Holding of share options could be relevant to the determination of a non-executive director's independence (as set out in provision A.3.1).

B.1.4 Where a company releases an executive director to serve as a nonexecutive director elsewhere, the remuneration report12 should include a statement as to whether or not the director will retain such earnings and, if so, what the remuneration is.

Service Contracts and Compensation

B.1.5 The remuneration committee should carefully consider what compensation commitments (including pension contributions and all other elements) their directors' terms of appointment would entail in the event of early termination. The aim should be to avoid rewarding poor performance. They should take a robust line on reducing compensation to reflect departing directors' obligations to mitigate loss.

B.1.6 Notice or contract periods should be set at one year or less. If it is necessary to offer longer notice or contract periods to new directors recruited from outside, such periods should reduce to one year or less after the initial period.

B.2 Procedure

Main Principle

There should be a formal and transparent procedure for developing policy on executive remuneration and for fixing the remuneration packages of individual directors. No director should be involved in deciding his or her own remuneration.

Supporting Principles

The remuneration committee should consult the chairman and/or chief executive about their proposals relating to the remuneration of other executive directors. The remuneration committee should also be responsible for appointing any consultants in respect of executive involved in advising or supporting the remuneration committee, care should be taken to recognise and avoid conflicts of interest. The chairman of the board should ensure that the company maintains contact as required with its principal shareholders about remuneration in the same way as for other matters.

Code Provisions

B.2.1 The board should establish a remuneration committee of at least three, or in the case of smaller companies two, members, who should all be independent non-executive directors. The remuneration committee should make available its terms of reference, explaining its role and the authority delegated to it by the board. Where remuneration consultants are appointed, a statement should be made available of whether they have any other connection with the company.

B.2.2 The remuneration committee should have delegated responsibility for setting remuneration for all executive directors and the chairman, including pension rights and any compensation payments. The committee should also recommend and monitor the level and structure of remuneration for senior management. The definition of 'senior management' for this purpose should be determined by the board but should normally include the first layer of management below board level.

B.2.3 The board itself or, where required by the Articles of Association, the shareholders should determine the remuneration of the non-executive directors within the limits set in the Articles of Association. Where permitted by the Articles, the board may however delegate this responsibility to a committee, which might include the chief executive.

B.2.4 Shareholders should be invited specifically to approve all new long-term incentive schemes (as defined in the Listing Rules) and significant changes to existing schemes, save in the circumstances permitted by the Listing Rules.

C. ACCOUNTABILITY AND AUDIT

C.1 Financial Reporting

Main Principle

The board should present a balanced and understandable assessment of the company's position and prospects.

Supporting Principle

The board's responsibility to present a balanced and understandable assessment extends to interim and other price-sensitive public reports and reports to regulators as well as to information required to be presented by statutory requirements.

Code Provisions

C.1.1 The directors should explain in the annual report their responsibility for preparing the accounts and there should be a statement by the auditors about their reporting responsibilities.

C.1.2 The directors should report that the business is a going concern, with supporting assumptions or qualifications as necessary.

C.2 Internal Control

Main Principle

The board should maintain a sound system of internal control to safeguard shareholders' investment and the company's assets.

Code Provision

C.2.1 The board should, at least annually, conduct a review of the effectiveness of the group's system of internal controls and should report to shareholders that they have done so. The review should cover all material controls, including financial, operational and compliance controls and risk management systems.

C.3 Audit Committee and Auditors

Main Principle

The board should establish formal and transparent arrangements for considering how they should apply the financial reporting and internal control principles and for maintaining an appropriate relationship with the company's auditors.

Code provisions

C.3.1 The board should establish an audit committee of at least three, or in the case of smaller companies two, members, who should all be independent non-executive directors. The board should satisfy itself that at least one member of the audit committee has recent and relevant financial experience.

C.3.2 The main role and responsibilities of the audit committee should be set out in written terms of reference and should include: to monitor the integrity of the financial statements of the company, and any formal announcements relating to the company's financial performance, reviewing significant financial reporting judgements contained in them; to review the company's internal financial controls and, unless expressly addressed by a separate board risk committee composed of independent directors, or by the board itself, to review the company's internal control and risk management systems; to monitor and review the effectiveness of the company's internal audit function; to make recommendations to the board, for it to put to the shareholders for their approval in general meeting, in relation to the appointment, re-appointment and removal of the external auditor and to approve the remuneration and terms of engagement of the external auditor; to review and monitor the external auditor's independence and objectivity and the effectiveness of the audit process, taking into consideration relevant UK professional and regulatory requirements; to develop and implement policy on the engagement of the external auditor to supply non-audit services, taking into account relevant ethical guidance regarding the provision of non-audit services by the external audit firm; and to report to the board, identifying any matters in respect of which it considers that action or improvement is needed and making recommendations as to the steps to be taken.

C.3.3 The terms of reference of the audit committee, including its role and the authority delegated to it by the board, should be made available. A separate section of the annual report should describe the work of the committee in discharging those responsibilities.

C.3.4 The audit committee should review arrangements by which staff of the company may, in confidence, raise concerns about possible improprieties in matters of financial reporting or other matters. The audit committee's objective should be to ensure that arrangements are in place for the proportionate and independent investigation of such matters and for appropriate follow-up action.

C.3.5 The audit committee should monitor and review the effectiveness of the internal audit activities. Where there is no internal audit function, the audit committee should consider annually whether there is a need for an internal audit function and make a recommendation to the board, and the reasons for the absence of such a function should be explained in the relevant section of the annual report.

C.3.6 The audit committee should have primary responsibility for making a recommendation on the appointment, reappointment and removal of the external auditors. If the board does not accept the audit committee's recommendation, it should include in the annual report, and in any papers recommending appointment or re-appointment, a statement from the audit committee explaining the recommendation and should set out reasons why the board has taken a different position.

C.3.7 The annual report should explain to shareholders how, if the auditor provides non-audit services, auditor objectivity and independence is safeguarded.

D. RELATIONS WITH SHAREHOLDERS

D.1 Dialogue with Institutional Shareholders

Main Principle

There should be a dialogue with shareholders based on the mutual understanding of objectives. The board as a whole has responsibility for ensuring that a satisfactory dialogue with shareholders takes place.

Supporting Principles

Whilst recognising that most shareholder contact is with the chief executive and finance director, the chairman (and the senior independent director and other directors as appropriate) should maintain sufficient contact with major shareholders to understand their issues and concerns. The board should keep in touch with shareholder opinion in whatever ways are most practical and efficient.

Code Provisions

D.1.1 The chairman should ensure that the views of shareholders are communicated to the board as a whole. The chairman should discuss governance and strategy with major shareholders. Non-executive directors should be offered the opportunity to attend meetings with major shareholders and should expect to attend them if requested by major shareholders. The senior independent director should attend sufficient meetings with a range of major shareholders to listen to their views in order to help develop a balanced understanding of the issues and concerns of major shareholders.

D.1.2 The board should state in the annual report the steps they have taken to ensure that the members of the board, and in particular the non-executive directors, develop an understanding of the views of major shareholders about their company, for example through direct face-to-face contact, analysts' or brokers' briefings and surveys of shareholder opinion.

D.2 Constructive Use of the AGM

Main Principle

The board should use the AGM to communicate with investors and to encourage their participation.

Code Provisions

D.2.1 The company should count all proxy votes and, except where a poll is called, should indicate the level of proxies lodged on each resolution, and the balance for and against the resolution and the number of abstentions, after it has been dealt with on a show of hands. The company should ensure that votes cast are properly received and recorded.

D.2.2 The company should propose a separate resolution at the AGM on each substantially separate issue and should in particular propose a resolution at the AGM relating to the report and accounts.

D.2.3 The chairman should arrange for the chairmen of the audit, remuneration and nomination committees to be available to answer questions at the AGM and for all directors to attend.

D.2.4 The company should arrange for the Notice of the AGM and related papers to be sent to shareholders at least 20 working days before the meeting.

APPENDIX 5 - EXTRACTS FROM 'MODERNISING COMPANY LAW: THE GOVERNMENT'S POLICY' (XXXX)

3 Improving Governance: Directors

3.1 A company is an abstract entity which can act only through individuals. This section of the text sets out the Government's proposals on directors, their duties and how their activities are regulated and monitored in the interests of the company.

Directors' Duties

General Duties Owed to the Company

3.2 The Act contains many specific provisions about responsibilities of directors. A company's constitution will also define their functions. But general rules about directors' propriety of conduct and standards of skill and care are laid down by complex and inaccessible case law. The duties are not therefore readily accessible to the layman. Indeed, a 1999 survey of members of the Institute of Directors showed that many company directors were not clear about what their general duties were or to whom they were owed.

3.3 The Review considered to whom directors should owe duties and consulted on this issue on several occasions. Its conclusion, with which the Government agrees, was that the basic goal for directors should be the success of the company in the collective best interests of shareholders, but that that directors should also recognise, as the circumstances require, the company's need to foster relationships with its employees, customers and suppliers, its need to maintain its business reputation, and its need to consider the company's impact on the community and the working environment.

3.4 The Review, building on the recommendations of a 1999 report by the Law Commissions, *Company Directors: Regulating Conflicts of Interest and Formulating a Statement of Duties*, recommended the codification of directors' common law duties - though without changing the essential nature of those duties - and the Final Report included a draft statutory statement restating the general principles governing the conduct of directors.

3.5 The Government agrees that:

- directors' general duties to the company should be codified in statute largely as proposed in the Final Report - but with some changes, explained in paragraphs 3.8 - 3.14 below. This statement of duties will replace the existing common law and also section 309 of the Act;

- the basic objective of directors, and the matters to which they should have regard when acting in furtherance of it, should be broadly as described in paragraph 3.3 above; and

- all the directors of a company should be subject to the same set of general duties, regardless of any particular duties they might have under service agreements as employees.

3.6 This approach - reflected in the draft at Schedule 2 in Volume II, which is essentially the version in the Review's Final Report (except for the removal of the final two paragraphs it had suggested - see 3.8 et seq. below) - balances a number of different elements. In particular, the duty in paragraph 2 of the Schedule to the draft Bill makes clear that directors must consider both the short and long term consequences of their actions, where relevant, and take into account where practicable relevant matters such as their relationships with employees and the impact of the business on the community and on the environment. At the same time the reference to practicability recognises that business decisions are often constrained by time limits or by the availability of information. In addition, the draft duties make clear that a director must exercise the care, skill and diligence of a reasonably diligent person with both the knowledge, skill and experience which may reasonably be expected of a director in his or her position and any additional knowledge, skill and experience which the particular director has.

3.7 The Government is currently considering how the text of the draft duties might be improved, and will consult in detail on a revised draft in due course. We would therefore welcome any detailed comments respondents may have on the drafting of clause 19 and Schedule 2 in Volume II, particularly from practitioners and those currently occupying the position of company director.

Question 1: (i) Does the draft statutory statement provide clear and authoritative guidance for directors?

(ii) Does it strike the right balance between modern business needs and wider expectations of responsible business behaviour?

Directors' Duties in Relation to Creditors

3.8 The Review proposed incorporating in the statutory statement a duty based on section 214 of the Insolvency Act 1986 which provides that where a company has gone into liquidation, the court, on the application of the liquidator, can declare that the director should make a contribution to its assets if, once there was no reasonable prospect of avoiding insolvency, he failed to take every step with a view to minimising the potential loss to the company's creditors.

3.9 In addition, it raised the possibility of also including a duty on directors in circumstances where the company was likely to become insolvent which would require them to strike a balance between the risk of the company becoming insolvent and promoting its success for the benefit of the members. However, the Review acknowledged fears that a duty framed in this way would "have a 'chilling effect', bringing with it the risk that directors may run down or abandon a going concern at the first hint of insolvency". It concluded that the advantages and disadvantages of such a principle were finely balanced and did not reach a final view on the point.

3.10 The Government has carefully considered both suggestions but has concluded in both cases that the weight of the argument is against the inclusion of any duties in relation to creditors in the statutory statement.

3.11 As noted above, the arguments against the retention of the second suggestion were outlined by the Review itself. Directors would need to take a finely balanced judgement, and fears of personal liability might lead to excessive caution. This would run counter to the 'rescue culture' which the Government is seeking to promote through the Insolvency Act 2000 and the Enterprise Bill now before Parliament.

3.12 The inclusion of a special duty where there is no reasonable prospect of avoiding insolvency was suggested mainly for presentational reasons. It was not intended to alter the law (although arguably it might result in some improvement or clarification at the margins). It would, however, de-couple the obligations imposed by section 214 of the Insolvency Act 1986 from the remedies under that Act in the case of registered companies. Its inclusion in the statutory statement would therefore be incongruous, particularly given that the Government is proposing to provide a comprehensive code of remedies in the Bill for all of the other the duties in the Schedule.

3.13 It is important to emphasise that there is no question about the need for section 214; but to incorporate it in the statement would unhelpfully conflate company and insolvency law. Directors have duties and obligations under many headings apart from company law (for example in relation to health and safety). The Government does not believe it appropriate to single out one requirement from insolvency law and include it within the codification of common law duties owed by directors to companies. To the extent that these obligations need to be drawn to directors' attention, it is considered that the comprehensive guidance on directors' statutory duties referred to in paragraph 3.17 below should include references to relevant provisions in the insolvency legislation.

3.14 An alternative approach to the question of creditors might be to include mention of them, perhaps by reference to the company's obligations to them, in the notes setting out the factors which, where they are relevant, directors must take into account in complying with duty in paragraph 2 of Schedule 2 in Volume II. The Government believes that this proposal is worth further consideration. However, such an approach would not achieve the effect intended by the Review in putting forward the duty in paragraph 8 of the Schedule included in the Review's Final Report.

Question 2: Would it be appropriate to include mention of creditors, perhaps by reference to the company's obligations to them, in the notes setting out the factors which, where they are relevant, directors must take into account in complying with the paragraph 2 duty?

How Should Directors Be Made Aware of Their Duties?

3.15 The Review recommended that directors should be required to sign a statement to the effect that they had read and understood the statutory statement of duties. There are obvious attractions in drawing the new, codified statement to all directors' attention in this way. However, it could also give a false impression that it was a comprehensive statement of directors' responsibilities. For example, it would not cover directors' obligations to make returns to Companies House.

3.16 There are also some technical problems with the Review's approach. The duties would be binding whether or not directors sign the statement, so signing would have no significant legal effect.

3.17 The Government therefore proposes instead to build on the current practice of Companies House of sending all new directors a leaflet setting out the requirements on directors to file accounts, make returns and provide other information to Companies House. In future all new directors would receive plain language guidance (also available in minority languages) summarising the main legal requirements placed on directors by company and insolvency legislation. This guidance would cover the statutory statement of duties, requirements to provide information to Companies House, and key provisions in the Bill such as the prohibition on fraudulent trading, as well as relevant aspects of insolvency law. It could be produced in a similar format to employment law guidance (and also made available on the web, through Business Links etc). There could be at least two versions of the guidance, one aimed at directors of (mostly smaller) private companies and another at directors of public companies.

Codification of Civil Remedies for Breach of Directors' Duties

3.18 The Review suggested that it would also be desirable to codify civil remedies for breach of directors' duties, although it noted that this is a difficult and complex area of law. If a workable scheme can be devised, the Government will publish draft clauses for consultation.

Directors' Conflicts of Interests

3.19 Part X of the Act underpins a director's fiduciary duties to his company by regulating possible conflicts of interest. The provisions were introduced to tackle abuses which the general law had failed to prevent.

3.20 The Government shares the overall approach recommended by the Review, which built on a report from the Law Commissions (see paragraph 3.4). We will consult on draft clauses in this area in due course.

Payments to Directors

3.21 One of the most significant and obvious conflicts of interest which directors face is in the setting of their remuneration. The current Table A provides that the board may determine the remuneration of the managing and executive directors. The Government agrees this is the right approach, and also believes that it is essential that there is effective disclosure and accountability to shareholders in this area.

3.22 The Government issued a consultative document in July 1999 which made a number of recommendations with a view to strengthening transparency and accountability in this area in respect of quoted companies. A further consultation document was issued in December 2001, inviting comments on the details of these proposals. We have subsequently laid a statutory instrument before Parliament which, when it comes into force, will require quoted companies to:

- publish a report on directors' remuneration as part of the company's annual reporting cycle;

- disclose within the report details of individual directors' remuneration packages, the company's remuneration policy, and the role of the board and remuneration committee in this area; and

- put an annual resolution to shareholders on the remuneration report.

3.23 The Government does not believe that it is appropriate to require such a formal approval procedure in respect of unquoted companies. Political Donations by Companies

3.24 Directors may also face a conflict of interest over political donations by companies, since a director's personal wishes or interests may conflict with his duty to the company. For that reason, the Act requires both the disclosure of donations in excess of £200 and - in line with a recommendation by the Committee on Standards in Public Life - prior shareholder authorisation of political donations above an annual threshold of £5,000.

3.25 The Government intends, for the most part, to retain in the Bill the recent amendments to the Act made by the Political Parties, Elections and Referendums Act 2000. It will, however, consider the case for further amendments in the light of the experience of companies and their members in implementing the new requirements and will consult on any proposals for changes in due course.

The Role of Codes of Best Practice

3.26 Operating at a number of levels, the corporate governance framework in Great Britain affects the ways in which directors run companies. There are some areas - particularly those relating to conflicts of interest - where Parliament has taken the view that it is appropriate to impose requirements on companies. In other areas, again primarily relating to conflicts of interest, the Listing Authority has imposed requirements on listed companies.

3.27 There is also, however, widespread agreement that there is an important role for a generally accepted code of best practice; in the United Kingdom, the Combined Code on Corporate Governance has fulfilled this role since 1998. There are, in addition, some areas where institutional investors have chosen to supplement the Combined Code with their own best practice guidance. Examples include the policy document Responsible Voting which was issued jointly by the Association of British Insurers and the National Association of Pension Funds in 1999.

3.28 The consensus that emerged from those who commented to the Review was that it would be unhelpful or inappropriate to put the provisions of the Combined Code into legislation. The main reasons given were that the case for flexibility in company governance structures was very strong; the definitional problems in the field were very severe; and shareholder control was a more appropriate mechanism for regulating such matters.

3.29 The Government believes that all the components of the corporate governance framework will continue to be important. In particular, it takes the view that, whilst legislative and regulatory requirements have an essential role, there will also be a continuing need for a code of best practice and other guidance. There is also a vital need for regular, systematic contact between directors and shareholders.

3.30 The Combined Code derives its strength from the widespread support which it has received from business and City organisations. The Government believes that it is very important that the Code continues to have this broad business and City support. (Responsibility for future reviews of the Code is discussed in paragraphs 5.11 - 5.13 below.)

3.31 The Review examined some areas covered by the Code. In particular, it considered the role of non-executive directors. The Government believes that nonexecutive directors can play a key role in the governance of companies, both in respect of accountability and business prosperity. It has therefore asked Derek Higgs to build on the work of the Review and of the Myners report on institutional investors by undertaking a short, independent review of the role and effectiveness of non-executive directors in the UK.

Corporate Directors

3.32 At present any legal person can be a company director - an individual, another company, a limited liability partnership, a local authority, etc. The only prohibition is on individuals of unsound mind, although minors are technically not capable of signing the requisite consent. At present about 2 per cent of all directors, i.e. about 64,000, are corporate bodies.

3.33 Few countries other than the Netherlands and some offshore financial centres permit corporate directors on the same basis as individuals. Some, for example Australia, New Zealand, Canada and Singapore, have only recently introduced prohibitions. France permits corporate directors but requires each to appoint an individual as its permanent representative with whom it is jointly responsible for any misconduct or negligence. Most US states, including Delaware and Maryland, require directors to be individuals.

3.34 A corporate director can act only through one or more individuals who represent it, or otherwise act on its behalf. The duties of directors need to apply to such individuals - and they need to know that they apply. If the directors are not individuals it can be difficult - both for the general public and for regulators - to determine who is actually controlling a company. Moreover, it can be difficult to apply sanctions against corporate directors. The Government believes that there would be real benefits and relatively little inconvenience from prohibiting corporate directors. It therefore proposes to:

- prohibit corporate directors for companies formed under the Bill;
- prohibit the appointment of corporate directors to existing companies; and
- after a transitional period of, say, three years, prohibit all corporate directors.

3.35 This issue was not addressed during the course of the Review, and we would welcome views.

Question 3: Do you agree that, subject to the transitional provisions described, corporate directors should be prohibited?

APPENDIX 6 - INDEX OF KEY WORDS

I

J

K

L

P

Packard, D - *28*
Parmalat - *20, 127*
personal mastery - *91*
perspective - *65, 85, 93*
Pope John Paul II - *28*
power - *6, 13, 21, 25, 30, 32, 50, 55, 56, 58, 63, 75, 76, 77, 78, 79, 80, 81, 82, 83, 85, 88, 90, 91, 92, 93, 94, 95, 96, 100, 101, 102, 106, 111, 112, 113, 126, 128, 130, 144*
Product Liability Law - *121*
property rights - *16, 50, 133*
prudence - *13, 14, 21, 70*
public trust - *43, 44, 45, 47, 48, 49, 50, 51, 53*

R

Reagan, R - *10, 138*
Registrar of Companies - *36*
registration - *35, 39*
regulation - *1, 10, 11, 12, 30, 43, 44, 72, 101, 115, 116, 117, 121, 122, 124, 128, 131, 132*
reserved powers - *93, 103*
responsibility - *2, 3, 5, 11, 16, 17, 20, 24, 38, 41, 46, 50, 54, 55, 61, 64, 70, 72, 74, 75, 80, 83, 86, 87, 88, 97, 101, 102, 112, 116, 118, 122, 134, 135, 136, 141, 143, 151, 152, 154, 162*
right relationships - *51, 101*
risk - *1, 14, 24, 31, 32, 36, 40, 44, 50, 65, 68, 70, 72, 81, 101, 106, 107, 108, 113, 121, 122, 123, 127, 135, 137, 142, 149, 152, 153, 158*
risk assessment - *81, 122, 137*
Robert Taylor Holdings - *71, 137*
role of CEO and chairman - *93*
Royal Bank of Scotland - *11*
Russia Company - *25*

S

Sarbannes Oxley Act - *127*
Schon, D - *97, 140*
Schwartz, P - *98, 140*
secrecy - *47, 51, 55, 63, 133*
selflessness - *48*
Senge, P - *83, 90, 140*